The Music of Vivian Fine

Heidi Von Gunden

The Scarecrow Press, Inc.
Lanham, Maryland, and London
1999

SCARECROW PRESS, INC.

Published in the United States of America
by Scarecrow Press, Inc.
4720 Boston Way
Lanham, Maryland 20706

4 Pleydell Gardens, Folkestone
Kent CT20 2DN, England

British Library Cataloguing in Publication Information Available

Library of Congress Cataloging-in-Publication Data

Von Gunden, Heidi, 1940–
   The music of Vivian Fine / Heidi Von Gunden.
     p. cm.
   Discography.
   Includes bibliographical references and index.
   ISBN 0-8108-3617-3 (cloth : alk. paper)
   1. Fine, Vivian, 1913– 2. Fine, Vivian, 1913—Criticism and
interpretation. 3. Composers—United States—Biography. I. Title.
ML410.F449V66   1999
780′.92—dc21
[b]   98-49550
                                            CIP
                                           MN

In memory of my mother, Evangeline Von Gunden

Contents

Preface

The music of Vivian Fine spans most of the twentieth century. Her first piece was composed in 1926 as an assignment for her theory teacher, Ruth Crawford. Her last piece, the *Memoirs of Uliana Rooney,* an opera about a feisty feminist composer, was written in 1994.

I met Vivian Fine in 1972, when Pauline Oliveros invited her to speak at the weekly forums for the music students at the University of California, San Diego. Fine, then a middle-aged woman with short bobbed hair, spoke about her music and played Henry Cowell's *Banshee.* I knew she taught at Bennington College, and both Oliveros and Fine seemed to enjoy the fact that Fine did not even have a high school diploma. I was fascinated by this woman and her music.

Later, when I became a faculty member at the University of Illinois at Champaign-Urbana, I invited Fine to speak at our Composers' Forum, an event with a reputation for being confrontational. I warned Fine—she replied: "Don't worry." She discussed her music and played part of *Momenti.* Afterward, I remarked to a colleague about the absence of arguments at the forum, and his reply was "That's because her music was so good!" Later I discovered that Fine had experience with similar situations—she was the only woman in Copland's Young Composers' Group.

Having studied and written about other composers, I wanted to understand more about Vivian Fine and her music. I began biweekly telephone interviews with her and was able to obtain most of her music, since her sister Adelaide Fine produces facsimile copies through Catamount Press. I learned about Fine's prodigious talent and her successful teenage years with support from Ruth Crawford, Henry Cowell, Dane Rudhyar, and others. As a young woman Fine was showing all the signs of a successful composer: Her music was performed in Chicago, New York, Germany, and South America; she was reviewed; and Cowell published some of her scores in *New Music.* I admired her courage to leave Chicago to live in New York City, where she earned her living as dance accompanist for such groups as Gluck-Sandor's and Doris Humphrey's. She had a family life, too. Vivian and Ben Karp were married in 1935 and had two daughters.

Yet Fine experienced obstacles as a woman composer. There were many times when she felt she was alone and removed from musical activity, and it was not until she was fifty-six years old that Fine was hired as a faculty member at Bennington College. Her position, at first, was half time. She taught piano and some composition.

However, composing has always been Fine's joy, and she never stopped, as is evident by her extensive catalog. Although she made certain her pieces were performed, she never actively promoted her music until 1973, when she decided to have an all-Fine concert at Finch Hall in New York City. Afterward her career blossomed, and she retired from Bennington in 1987 because she needed more time to complete her commissions.

Fine's life and music form a fascinating story, which she and Sonya Freidman portray in the chamber opera, *Memoirs of Uliana Rooney* (1994). Fine was especially interesting to me because she is several months younger than my mother, Evangeline, whom I was taking care of during the last stages of her debilitating illness while writing this book. Both Vivian and Evangeline shared some of the excitements and tragedies of the twentieth century. This book is dedicated to Evangeline's memory.

Last, I would like to thank the University of Illinois for a Research Award that enabled me to have an assistant prepare the musical examples for this book. Lori Jones did this work and was a wonderful aid in locating reviews and other material.

Chapter 1

The Early Years

On September 28, 1913, David and Rose Fine gave birth to their second daughter, Vivian. The baby girl had an older sister, Adelaide, who was born in 1910, and the next year, 1914, Vivian would have another sister, Eleanor (see fig. 1.1). Both David and Rose were Russian-Jewish immigrants. David was born in Latvia and came to the United States when he was eight years old. The family stayed in New York for awhile, but then moved to Chicago. Rose Finder was from the Ukraine, although she did not remember much about her Russian heritage since her family settled in Chicago when she was two years old. Rose was a bright young woman who by age fourteen was employed as a full-time secretary trained in shorthand and typing. Earlier she had received a piano as a gift from her sister, Bertha, who paid for it with monthly installments of fifty cents from her meager salary as a worker in a cigar-making factory. Rose learned to play the piano, but the instrument was to become an important part in Vivian's life. Rose had a good job at Sears Roebuck, and later a coworker introduced her to David Fine. They married when Rose was twenty and David was twenty-five and lived on the West side of Chicago in an improvised Jewish ghetto.[1]

David had only a third-grade education but eventually became box office manager of the Yiddish theater in Chicago and later manager of a furniture store. Typical of his Jewish heritage, David had great respect for learning and believed in self-education through reading. He encouraged his daughters to do so likewise. Part of this education was attending lectures, some of which were related to his socialist politics and others to cultural matters in general. At times his daughters attended, and Vivian remembers hearing Bertrand Russell speak.[2]

Rose Fine had an even greater impact upon her daughter. The three-year-old Vivian was fascinated by her mother's piano, which was now housed at her Aunt Bertha's. Vivian recalls that she "was enchanted by the sound."[3] In fact, the instrument seemed to have such an effect on the child that she surprised her parents by having a tantrum, declaring that she

Figure 1.1.   Eleanor, Adelaide, and Vivian (*right*), Chicago, 1917.

wanted to learn how to play the piano.[4] Considering young Vivian to be even tempered, Rose took her child's request seriously and had the piano moved to their house. At first Rose taught her daughter, but it soon became apparent that she should hire a piano teacher. Although the family was poor—Vivian stated: "We were at the poverty level, not near it, but at it"[5]—music lessons were a worthwhile expense, and Adelaide was already taking violin lessons. However, there was one problem with young Vivian—Miss Rosen, the neighborhood piano teacher, only accepted students age eight and above. This did not stop Rose Fine; she invited Miss Rosen to hear Vivian play. The rule was bent, and Vivian was accepted as a student. Apparently Miss Rosen was a strict teacher because Vivian remembers that "she had a curious method of correcting wrong notes—if I played a wrong note, she hit me on the hand with a fly swatter."[6]

The lessons lasted for about two or three months, because Rose Fine had another idea for her daughter. She took Vivian to the Chicago Musical College to audition for a scholarship. Again Vivian's age was a drawback. The faculty at the Chicago Musical College did not believe that Vivian was five because she was quite tall. Undeterred, Rose went to City Hall and got a copy of Vivian's birth certificate as proof of the child's age.[7] The scholarship was awarded, and Vivian studied with Helen Ross for three years.

Apparently, although this teacher was conscientious, Vivian needed better instruction, so between ages nine and ten she studied with a Mr. Weinstein and a Mr. Lempkoff. For a short time it appeared that Vivian might be destined for a career as a violinist because Adelaide's violin teacher, a Mr. Fiedler, discovered that Vivian had perfect pitch. However, the lessons were not too successful because Vivian is left-handed.

Meanwhile Vivian attended Theodor Herzl Grammar School and participated in the childhood activities in her Jewish neighborhood. Naturally, music was a large part of her life, and together with her two sisters she would listen to the family's windup phonograph, enjoying hearing recordings by such singers as Enrico Caruso and Geraldine Farrar.

By age eleven, Vivian's music study was further accelerated when she became a pupil of Djane Lavoie-Herz, a prominent musician in the Chicago area. Vivian remembers Madame Herz as "flamboyant—she was a real personality."[8] A former pupil of Scriabin, she was a devotee of his music and philosophy. Madame Herz was interested in promoting her students, and even arranged for Vivian to present a recital at the home of some socially prominent friends in the Chicago area.

Ruth Crawford, who at this time was in her early twenties, was also a student of Madame Herz. Ruth knew Henry Cowell, Dane Rudhyar, Imre Weisshaus, and others who attended the salons that Madame Herz held at her house. Probably it was Ruth who introduced Vivian to Cowell, Rudhyar, and Weisshaus.[9] Rudhyar, who soon took an interest in this young woman's musical talent, wrote these inspiring words to her: "You have so much within you! Let it grow and develop—and do not forget your old friend who believes in you and your great power of expression."[10]

Vivian looked up to Ruth as a role model of a young woman who was serious about being a musician. Since at this time Ruth was attending the American Conservatory of Music and studying composition and theory with John Palmer and Adolf Weidig, Madame Herz suggested that Ruth teach Vivian theory and in return Madame Herz would not charge Ruth for her piano lessons. Vivian was delighted. Ruth assigned some exercises from Weidig's text, *Harmonic Material and Its Uses*.[11] Vivian was the ideal student according to this text, because she had natural talent, which Weidig described this way: "Talent means being endowed with an ear capable of development into a discriminating ear; a sense of musical logic; and, further, the physical adaptability for the chosen instrument."[12] Earlier Vivian had been identified as having perfect pitch, Weidig's "discriminating ear," and unlike Ruth and Madame Herz, who both had muscular problems related to piano performance,[13] Fine never experienced such difficulties, thus possessing "the physical adaptability for the chosen instrument." It was not long before the theory lessons took another direction.

Ruth composed music, and as part of the theory instruction asked Vivian to write a short piece. She returned with a piano composition, and this assignment changed the direction of her life. Later Fine recalled: "The unfortunate thing for Madame Herz was that I became so interested in composition that I neglected the piano."[14]

The young Vivian began to neglect something else, too. She found her freshman year in high school boring and taking too much time away from her study of music. Mrs. Fine agreed that high school seemed like a waste for her talented daughter and approved of her quitting school. After all, it was at about the same age that Rose went to work as a professional secretary, and the Jewish family tradition placed such stress on self-education through reading and private study that she was certain her daughter would further her intellectual life. Apparently the truant officer investigated Vivian's absence from school, and Mrs. Fine solved the problem by hiding Vivian in a closet. In her eighties Vivian remembered her mother fondly, stating, "I appreciated what she did for me, always."[15]

Although Vivian attended concerts, taking advantage of student tickets for the Saturday night performances of the Chicago Symphony, she was fascinated by the avant garde music of the late twenties, which was featured at the performances at Madame Herz's salon. Vivian was eager to study scores and would frequent the Lyon & Healy music store in Chicago, looking at music by Hindemith, Schoenberg, and others. Occasionally she had enough money to buy a score, and she subscribed to Cowell's *New Music*.[16] She also devoted some of her piano practice to learning Schoenberg's *Opus 19,* the easier pieces of *Opus 11,* and some of Ruth Crawford's music, probably the *Nine Preludes* (1924–28) and the *Study in Mixed Accents* (1929).

It was about this time, too, that Crawford's *Sonata for Violin and Piano* (1926) was premièred at a recital held at the Cliff House in Chicago. Vivian was there, and Ruth gave her a manuscript copy of the piece. This impressed the young musician, who was eager to hear and study modern music. She treasured the gift, and years later was able to return the favor. Somehow Crawford's original was lost and the *Sonata* was unknown. Discovering this, in 1962 Fine gave her copy, the only surviving one, to the Library of Congress, and then in 1984, together with Ida Kavafian, Fine recorded the *Sonata* for Composers Recordings Incorporated (CRI SD 508).

It was not long before composing became a passion for Vivian. She wrote at the piano, using her keen ear to imagine what her piece would sound like. She never thought it strange that a woman should be writing music because Ruth did it. Many of her earlier pieces were written while she was studying with Ruth, but when Crawford left Chicago to study with Charles Seeger in New York, Vivian became heir to Ruth's scholarship to study with Weidig at the American Conservatory.[17] These were private composition lessons, but Vivian found that the pedagogue did not seem to understand her modernistic approach. For Vivian each piece was an experiment, trying out a new idea she had discovered. However, in 1929 Weidig did make it possible for Vivian to have her official debut as a composer. He held a student composition recital each year, and Fine premièred a *Sonatina* for violin and piano, a work that is not available for study.

Experimentation is apparent in her early piece, *Solo for Oboe* (1929). At the time she did not know an oboist, but liked the sound and decided to write for it. The piece is in three movements: Allegretto (quarter-note = 176), Lento (quarter-note = 72), and Con spirito (quarter-note = 126). Although it is not inscribed on this piece (she would do this later), the young composer was careful that an accidental affect only the note it precedes, and she added courtesy naturals to make her intentions clear. The *Solo for Oboe* is a study in energy as created by line and duration. For example, the line of movement one is a mixture of consonant and dissonant intervals marked by large leaps of a major seventh or minor ninth, which create energy that is released through a change in direction and narrower movement (see ex. 1.1).

Although it would seem that Fine was using motivic patterning (such as the B-A-F outlined in measures 1 and 3 of ex. 1.1) or intervalic control such as fourths followed by minor ninths, these are not significant, and on a number of occasions Fine stated: "I would not have been conscious of cells or motifs at that time. I just wrote intuitively."[18] However, she was aware of Charles Ruggles's method of not repeating a pitch or its octave until eight or ten other pitches had occurred, as is evident in example 1.1. The $D^{\sharp 5}$,[19] which begins *Solo for Oboe,* is repeated in measure 3 as $E^{\flat 4}$, exactly ten pitches away. But this was not a strict system for her, as can be seen by the repetition of A as A^5, just six notes away from the previous A. Fine recalled that she was not interested in creating a compositional system or procedure.[20] Instead, these were the kinds of sounds and durations that she was hearing in the modernistic works she admired, and it was material that appealed to her.

The form for movement one of *Solo for Oboe* is ternary, with the recapitulation containing several modifications and alterations of the initial

Example 1.1.   Line and energy in the first movement of *Solo for Oboe* (1929).

Example 1.2. Measures 23–35 of *Solo for Oboe* (1929) showing recapitulation and internal closure.

material, such as the circled measures in example 1.2 in which the beginning four notes are repeated, but the G♯ is stressed while the durations of the other pitches are changed to transform the phrase shape. Example 1.2 also illustrates how she created internal closure in measure 29 with longer durations and a line that ascends to the movement's highest point, E^6. Notice the silence that precedes and highlights this moment.

The other movements have similar ideas. The Lento's contrast is its long durations of dotted half-notes and even a double whole-note with dynamic fluctuations that shape phrases, such as the ending four measures in example 1.3.

The third movement is dancelike with a *con spirito* tempo of changing eighth-note meters and punctuated articulations (see ex. 1.4). References to the first and second movements' tempi and textures are heard at the midpoint with an allegretto and later eighth-note patterning heard as a recapitulation. *Solo for Oboe* cadences with the same G♯^{5} G^4 B^4 that ended movement one.

Fine composed *Solo for Oboe* when she was sixteen years old, and what is amazing are the varying phrase lengths, articulations, durational variety, and sense of recapitulation. Imre Weisshaus, one of Vivian's friends, thought so highly of the piece that he arranged for *Solo for Oboe* to be premièred on April 21, 1930, at a Pan-American Association of Composers' Concert at the Chamber Hall of Carnegie Hall in New York City.[21] Fine was unable to attend the concert because she could not afford the trip to New York, but there were other local occasions for performances of her music.

Example 1.3. Ending measures of Lento from *Solo for Oboe* (1929) showing durational contrast and dynamic variety.

Con spirito (♩ = 126)

Example 1.4.   Beginning measures of the third movement of *Solo for Oboe* (1929).

Naturally, having a New York première is encouraging for a young composer, and it would not be long before she would have an international première of another composition, *Four Pieces for Two Flutes* (1930).[22] The lines have a similar angular nature, avoidance of repeated pitches, and attention to articulations and dynamics as in the *Solo for Oboe,* but dissonance becomes more apparent due to the counterpoint. Fine was careful to contrast the two lines. Also, there are fewer meter changes, probably for ease of performance. Instead, durational interest is created by polyrhythms. The first piece is a play upon the relationship between the two flutes. At times flute one is the leader with a louder and more prominent line while the second flute's counterpoint accompanies (see ex. 1.5). Reversals occur, and at one point there is a canon at the octave. A recapitulation is heard in measure 43 but is soon altered because Fine was careful to avoid direct repetition. In addition to having an excellent ear, she was a careful craftsperson. In her words: "I worked hard on these compositions. It took me many years before I would consider repeating something exactly."[23]

The second piece reflects its "Lento tristo, eighth-note = 76" marking with chromatic lines featuring whole- or half-steps. The ending shown in example 1.6 illustrates the undulating cadences that become prominent in her later works.

Dissonance and activity become intense in the third piece, *Stridente*. The undulating action shown in example 1.6 becomes a trill in both voices in

Grazioso, un poco giocoso [♩ = 152]

Example 1.5.   Beginning measures of movement one of *Four Pieces for Two Flutes* (1930). (Copyright © 1981 by GunMar Music, Inc.; used with permission.)

Chapter 1

Example 1.6.   Undulating cadence to second piece of *Four Pieces for Two Flutes* (1930). (Copyright © 1981 by GunMar Music, Inc.; used with permission.)

example 1.7, a texture that will mark her future works. The energy generated in this example is abruptly cut off with a measure of silence. The contrast adds to the drama, and later Fine uses polyrhythms of three against five and three against four to create durational interest. Again, there is a sense of recapitulation in which ideas are recalled; however, subtle changes in pitch and duration make the closure interesting. Weisshaus, to whom Fine had sent a copy of her piece, praised this movement especially: "The 3rd movement is doubtless the best of the four, I believe. Even much more than that: I think it is one of the best compositions I have seen lately by American composers (this is not a compliment, merely a fact!)."[24]

The fourth piece returns to a light and delicate texture and a mood that resembles piece one (see ex. 1.8). Rhythms are simpler due to its dance-like character, and although Fine did not use rigid formal patterns, this piece has more repetition than in the previous ones, causing it to have a ternary shape. The beginning phrases are repeated twice in the A section

Example 1.7.   Beginning measures of the third piece of *Four Pieces for Two Flutes* (1930). (Copyright © 1981 by GunMar Music, Inc.; used with permission.)

Example 1.8. Beginning measures of the fourth piece of *Four Pieces for Two Flutes* (1930). (Copyright © 1981 by GunMar Music, Inc.; used with permission.)

with the repetition being "*vigoroso* and forte" while the original was "*delicato* and piano." The B section begins with a measure of silence, a characteristic that has marked her young work, and the return to the A section is recognizable but soon becomes varied and changed as in the other pieces.

Soon this piece received special attention. While Crawford was in Germany as a result of her Guggenheim Grant, an occasion arose to program Vivian's *Four Pieces for Two Flutes*. Fine had sent a copy to Weisshaus who then shared it with Ruth. In a letter to Vivian, Ruth explained, "I made a copy [of *Four Pieces for Two Flutes*] for the Hamburg jury, and must say it was a pleasure, in copying, to feel your growth, and to feel that you are gripping what you have to say with a firmer hand."[25]

The jury approved, and in April Vivian's piece was performed as *Four Pieces for Oboe and Violin* in a concert of music by women in Hamburg. Apparently no one consulted her about the change in instrumentation.[26] Crawford's *Diaphonic Suite No. 4* for viola and cello was also heard.[27] Fine and Crawford were the American representatives for this event. Again, Fine could not attend, but was grateful to have the performance.

The year of 1930 was busy for the young Fine. Her friend, Ruth, had moved to New York and in February wrote a lengthy letter giving the following advice:

And let me stress again in teacherly fashion the need for objective as well as subjective, for the composer. Know as much as you can. Knowing cannot hurt you. Not knowing for the sake of being brilliant, but knowing for the sake of being able to give more freely, with power and without useless effort. Study Forsythe, study other books on orchestration—Rimsky Korsakow [*sic*], Berlioz. Make a practice of reading quartet scores at the piano and away from the piano. Become familiar with clefs. You will thank yourself heartily ten years from now for the ease that will result. A composer has a hard enough time putting himself down in black and white, aside from the added difficulties of clefs and topsy-turvy transposition systems. Have you finished the Verklarte Nacht?

Don't misunderstand me. Of course the subjective is important, it is the essence. Music must flow. It must be a thread unwinding, a thread from no one knows just where. It must not be a problem in mathematics, writing music. Schonberg [*sic*] has grown too many geometric pages. But there is a balance. You need not polish the receptacle so meticulously that you have no energy left for filling it. Neither would I consider it complimentary to put a grand flow of sound into a rusty dishpan.[28]

In November and December Fine wrote an ambitious piece, *Trio in Three Movements for Violin, Viola and Violoncello* (1930). The *Trio* shows how rapidly Fine was mastering compositional techniques. Naturally, in comparison to *Solo for Oboe* and the *Four Pieces for Two Flutes,* the *Trio* is thicker, but it also has more interesting rhythms, such as quintuplets and polyrhythms of five against four and four against three as seen in example 1.9. Interestingly, Crawford had written suggesting that Fine practice scales in counter-rhythms, two against three, three against four, two against five, and so on, while paying attention to interesting off-accents that occur.[29] Perhaps Fine was realizing Crawford's suggestions in the *Trio*.

The form becomes more defined, as is apparent in the third movement's rondo. Material is shaped by motivic patterns that appear throughout the various counterpoints. In the first movement, these patterns are meant to be recognized because the opening six measures are heard in unison before a three-part texture begins in measure 9. Soon the texture thickens, and the motifs in the cello are counterpointed with a prominent viola melody with brackets to indicate a *haupt* motif and accompanimental figures in the first violin (see ex. 1.10).

There are several double stops, and at this time Fine did not have access to string players other than Adelaide, so Fine imagined what *Trio* would sound like. She did look at scores by Hindemith and Schoenberg for ideas. Contrast among the instruments is marked by changes in dynamic markings, labeling of solo passages, and *haupt* motifs (indicated with brackets),[30] which are shorter and more energetic material than that

Example 1.9.   Motivic and rhythmic patterning in the first movement of *Trio in Three Movements for Violin, Viola and Violoncello* (1930).

Example 1.10. *Haupt* motifs, figures, and expressive lines in the first movement of *Trio in Three Movements for Violin, Viola and Violoncello* (1930).

used in previous pieces. One suspects that the bracketing was probably influenced by her study of Schoenberg's scores.

The second movement, titled "Intermezzo," is a beautiful melody accompanied by a cello pizzicato ostinato. Later the melody is fragmented, passed among the instruments, heard doubled at the major seventh, and decorated before returning to a short recapitulation.

"Rondo," which is an *attacca* from the second movement, has a spirited motivic A section, a slower and more lyrical B section, and an imitative C section. The rondo pattern is not proportional—the second A is a three-measure remembrance of the original material; the C section is long and developmental; and the closing A is the same length as the original but, as is her custom, is not an exact repetition. With this movement Fine is moving closer to a more sophisticated writing. Material is recombined, echoed, and varied, and ideas are juxtaposed, as shown in example 1.11.

Example 1.11. Juxtaposition in measures 90–93 of "Rondo" from *Trio in Three Movements for Violin, Viola and Violoncello* (1930).

It was not long after *Trio* was composed that Fine began to make plans to move to New York, as Ruth had done earlier. Mrs. Fine supported the move, although she must have had some misgivings about a young woman alone in the big city. When discussing, in retrospect, what it was like to be a female composer during this time, Fine replied: "People had prejudices against women composers, but I did have enlightened people I was in touch with who took an interest in this very young person. They took me seriously."[31] They recognized talent.

NOTES

1. They were not practicing Jews, but rather subscribed to Jewish socialism, hopeful of improving working conditions for the immigrant Jewish working class. For more information about Jewish life at this time and Jewish socialism see Irving Howe, *World of Our Fathers* (New York: Harcourt Brace Jovanovich, 1976), especially Chapter 9, "Jewish Labor, Jewish Socialism," 287–324.

2. Author's telephone interview with Fine, June 3, 1994.

3. Author's telephone interview with Fine, December 10, 1993.

4. Janet Nichols in her book, *Women Music Makers: An Introduction to Women Composers* (New York: Walker and Co., 1992), 126–45, relates many of these early stories about Fine.

5. Author's telephone interview with Fine, December 10, 1993.

6. Author's telephone interview with Fine, December 10, 1993.

7. Author's telephone interview with Fine, December 10, 1993.

8. Author's telephone interview with Fine, December 10, 1993. See also, Judith Tick, *Ruth Crawford Seeger: A Composer's Search for American Music* (New York: Oxford University Press, 1997), 44–51.

9. Author's telephone interview with Fine, August 6, 1994.

10. Letter from Dane Rudhyar to Vivian Fine dated December 22, 1930. Used with Fine's permission.

11. Adolf Weidig, *Harmonic Material and Its Uses* (Chicago: Clayton F. Summy Co., 1923). Weidig's text was comprehensive, beginning with the fundamentals and ending with modulation and pedal point. It is also possible that Crawford and Fine used some of the materials from Weidig's *Modern Counterpoint,* which at that time would have been in manuscript form because the book was not published until 1936. It was available through Carl Fisher.

12. Weidig, *Harmonic Material,* 1.

13. According to Gaume, Ruth Crawford was plagued with muscular tightness, probably a condition that would be diagnosed today as carpal tunnel syndrome or tendinitis. (See Matilda Gaume, *Ruth Crawford Seeger: Memoirs, Memories, Music* [Metuchen, N.J.: Scarecrow Press, 1986].) Fine recalled that Madame Herz also had muscular problems. Author's telephone interview with Fine, December 10, 1993.

14. Author's telephone interview with Fine, May 20, 1994.

15. Author's telephone interview with Fine, December 17, 1993.

16. Rita Mead, *Henry Cowell's New Music 1925–1936: The Society, the Music Editions, and the Records* (Ann Arbor, Mich.: UMI Research Press, 1981), 126.

17. Apparently there was some doubt at first if Weidig would be allowed to take Vivian as a student. In a letter dated September 15, 1929, addressed to Vivian and her mother, Ruth Crawford mentioned that she had written Weidig and included a list of Vivian's compositions "in hopes he might be sufficiently impressed to move a mountain or two for your sakes." Crawford urged Vivian to try to see Weidig as soon as possible. Used with Fine's permission.

18. Author's telephone interview with Fine, June 3, 1994.

19. The register number is standardized international acoustical terminology. Middle C is C^4 and the numbers increase as the registers are higher. Each successive C begins a new register.

20. Author's telephone interview with Fine, February 9, 1995.

21. In Weisshaus's letter to Fine dated March 28, 1930, he confirms that her piece will be performed. Weisshaus closed his letter with the following: "You know how much I am interested in your work!" (used with Fine's permission). A short article in the *New York Times,* April 22, 1930, lists Fine's composition and the other works performed, which were Ruth Crawford's *Rat Riddles* (Crawford's name is omitted), Carlos Chávez's *Sonatina* for violin and piano, Cowell's *Indiana, New River,* and *Ann Street,* Weisshaus's *Six Pieces for Solo Voice,* and Alejandro Caturla's *Afro-Cuban Songs,* plus other short pieces by Rudhyar, Strang, Brant, Weiss, and Antheil.

22. Although Fine was prolific during her teen years, the next piece retained in her catalog is the *Four Pieces for Two Flutes.* This is the first piece available from GunMar Music, Inc.

23. Author's telephone interview with Fine, June 3, 1994.

24. Letter from Weisshaus to Fine dated August 23, 1931 (used with Fine's permission). Weisshaus was in Berlin at the time. He made several suggestions about *Four Pieces for Two Flutes,* such as having the C^4 of flute two in measure 1 of movement one transposed an octave higher. Most of his comments are about register and accidental choices, using a flat instead of a sharp, and so on. Fine never made the changes; however, one of Weisshaus's remarks became an important aspect of her later compositions. He recommended that when a theme is repeated, to shift it forwards or backwards by an eighth-note, a procedure she has often used since the 1970s.

25. Letter from Crawford to Fine dated June 13, 1931 (used with Fine's permission). However, apparently Ruth did not immediately think of including Fine's composition for the jury. In a letter to Fine from Virginia Weisshaus dated January 3, 1932 she related the following:

By the way, Vivian, Imre asked me to let you know about the Hamburg affair. When Ruth was living, as she did for a short time after I left for Dessau, in the same house with Imre, a man telephoned there who said he was from the Hamburg Chapter of the International Society for Contemporary Music and was looking for material for a concert of women composers. He had heard Ruth's work at the November Gruppe Concert, and wanted some of her things. She was very much excited of course, and during six days, was preparing and choosing and copying from her own compositions (among other things of course). Imre says he was watching her all the time, whether she would think of you at all, and finally on the 7th day, he said to her "Wouldn't this be a chance also for Vivian?" and she was quite shocked, and said, "Oh, of *course!*" and in a great hurry to make up for having forgotten it, she copied your piece herself, and sent it off with hers. You have probably heard from her that yours and one of hers was accepted.

The emphasis is Mrs. Weisshaus's.

26. Author's telephone interview with Fine, December 17, 1993.

27. Gaume, *Ruth Crawford Seeger,* 61.

28. Letter from Crawford to Fine dated February 7, 1930. Used with Fine's permission.

29. Letter from Crawford to Fine dated February 7, 1930. Crawford also mentioned that she would be sending a copy of Cowell's book, *New Musical Resources.*

30. Fine does not recall thinking of them as such. Her intention was to bring out a certain line. Author's telephone interview with Fine, July 1, 1994.

31. Author's telephone interview with Fine, May 20, 1994.

Chapter 2

New York and the 1930s

Although Fine's teenage years in Chicago were exciting, with prominent musicians interested in her musical career, in 1931 she moved to New York City because she needed further involvement with modern music. Fine recalls that she "went to New York on Ruth Crawford's advice and Madame Herz's, probably."[1] Rudhyar was encouraging, too, writing:

> What you need, more than [to] study rules and technique, is *to grow as a creative personality:* to gain self-assurance, self-knowledge and to experience many conditions of life. Modern music is up against a wall; and only the heroic soul will ever pierce through this wall and into the future. . . . One you know was given a chance and apparently did not succeed so well. But *you* are strong, and I trust you shall prove it—to yourself, whether or not others see it or approve of it.[2]

Cowell thought that Fine should study dissonant counterpoint with Charles Seeger, a direction that Crawford had taken. Frequently Fine sent Cowell her new compositions, which he shared with others, such as Rudhyar and Weisshaus. Cowell also was in correspondence with her and wrote this passage before she left for New York:

> These works which you have just sent, seem to be in your familiar style, but there is a distinct attempt to branch out, particularly in counterpoint. I think you should try to study dissonant counterpoint. The work shows a lack of apprehension, I think, of the specific details of dissonant counterpoint. The tessitura of your work is too low, and there is not enough arrival at some particular point, in the form as a whole.[3]

Naturally, Fine discussed the move with her parents, who were sympathetic, and the understanding was that since Vivian was such a good pianist, she could earn her living as a musician. Earlier Rudhyar cautioned: "The air is crowded with incoming events and much will take place within a few years. So be prepared to face all and to be able to stand on your own feet, and earn your own living."[4] Vivian would realize Rudhyar's prediction. Mr. and Mrs. Fine gave their daughter fifty dollars to establish herself in New York. It was the best they could do, and this was the last money Vivian ever took from them.[5]

In the fall of 1931 Fine left Chicago. Fortunately she had an aunt and uncle in New York City with whom she stayed for several days before finding a room in Greenwich Village. At first she "felt lost and lonesome,"[6] but it was not long before she met some kindred spirits—Crawford, who had returned from Europe and had just married Charles Seeger, Aaron Copland,[7] Joseph Schillinger, and others interested in modern music. In addition, there was an opportunity for Fine to present her compositions to the New York musical community. Cowell was influential in suggesting to Blanch Walton, a patroness of the arts, that she sponsor a recital of Fine's music, which would be held in Walton's home.[8] The same had been done for Ruth Crawford earlier. Fine remembers that many distinguished musicians were present, especially those who supported the avant garde.[9]

It was not long before Fine made an appointment with Seeger to begin composition study. Apparently she had one lesson, and that was all. In her words: "The idea [to move to New York] was to study with Charles Seeger, but it never took place. I don't know why, exactly."[10]

Locating work was important, and Fine auditioned for Gluck-Sandor, a choreographer who was combining ballet and modern dance in productions that he called Dance Theater. His Dance Center was to open in the fall of 1931, and he needed a dance accompanist, an accomplished pianist who could perform the piano reductions of such works as Stravinsky's *Petrushka* and Strauss's *Salome*. Fine auditioned at the studio, which was on top of a garage on West 54th Street. She performed one of Brahms's *Rhapsodies*.[11] When asked about her job qualifications, she implied that she was experienced as a dance accompanist, although she had only played for one dance class in Chicago. Her acute hearing coupled with excellent sight reading skills served her well. She got the job. It paid fifty cents an hour. The top dance accompanist salary at that time was $1.50.[12] That season they performed *Petrushka, Salome,* de Falla's *El Amor Brujo,* and Prokofiev's *Prodigal Son,* all accompanied by piano transcriptions that Fine played for rehearsals and performances. Gluck-Sandor could be difficult at times, and Fine found it annoying when he would stop the music in the middle of a phrase and insert a pause. In an interview, Fine recalled that Gluck-Sandor was "a little mad and he called me Madame X." [13] Also, he was not a reliable employer and eventually owed Fine fifty dollars in back salary.

Fine stayed in Greenwich Village only for a short time and then moved to a "cold water flat" in uptown on Perry Street, now fashionable east 50th Street. Since there was no hot water or heat, she used a toaster to keep warm. When the Thomas Edison man read the electric meter, his comment was "What are you running here—a factory?" because the bill was twenty-six dollars.[14] It was not long before that toaster took care of more than just Vivian. In February of 1932 her father lost his job in Chicago, so the Fines came to New York to live with Vivian, thus keeping the family together.

Meanwhile Fine was making a reputation as an excellent free-lance dance accompanist. Later Doris Humphrey, Charles Weidman, and Martha Graham employed Fine, also. In addition, they recognized her compositional skills and had her write music for their choreography.

But what Fine really wanted was to learn more about modern music, which she did through performance. She was the pianist for many concerts. She premièred Crawford's *Study in Mixed Accents* at a class Charles Seeger was teaching at the New School for Social Research in New York City and performed Carlos Chávez's *Sonata* (1924) for a concert series dedicated to contemporary music that Seeger presented at the New School. Copland assisted during the concert by turning pages. Unfortunately the new music performances did not add to her meager income—it was the Depression and artists were expected to perform for the love of it.

Copland saw the need for helping young musicians, especially composers, and formed the Young Composers' Group, which met in his apartment at the Empire Hotel.[15] Fine does not remember if she was there from the beginning,[16] but it was not long before she became one of the group, which consisted of Arthur Berger, Paul Bowles, Henry Brant, Israel Citkowitz, Lehman Engel, Vivian Fine, Irwin Heilner, Bernard Herrmann, Jerome Moross, and Elie Siegmeister.[17] Henry Brant, who later was a colleague of Fine's at Bennington, remembered that Fine was a vital member. "From time to time someone would bring in a piece perhaps unknown to all of us—something by Eisler, Ives, or Webern that we'd never seen before. We'd say 'Vivian, play it.' (Vivian was the best sight reader in the group.)"[18] Copland realized this, too, and had Fine play his *Piano Variations* while he proofread the music.[19]

The Young Composers' Group had lively discussions, apparently rarely coming to agreement, but it was important that these young people have an opportunity to meet because, as Fine recalls, "compared to today, there were very few composers. They [the Composers' Group] were it—the modern composers."[20] Obviously, Fine was the only woman and when asked about that, she replied, "I liked it!"[21] Being part of the group relieved her initial feelings of lonesomeness when she moved to New York. Vivian felt "they were all pals."[22] Frequently after a session, they went to a nearby cafeteria for dinner or lunch, which cost fifteen cents.

Copland included the Young Composers' Group in his plans for the First Yaddo Festival, and Fine's *Four Polyphonic Pieces for Piano* (1931–32)

Example 2.1. Imitation, tetrachordal motif, and conservative line in the beginning measures of "Moderato," the first piece of the *Four Polyphonic Pieces for Piano* (1931–32).

were to be on the program with Fine as pianist on April 30, 1932, the first day of the two-day festival.[23] She had begun them earlier in Chicago and completed the collection when she came to New York. The compositions are less free and more constricted than her previous music due to the counterpoint.[24]

In the first piece, "Moderato," the listener hears an imitative two-voiced counterpoint inverted at the interval of an augmented fifth that quickly thickens to three voices. The tetrachordal motif is obvious, and, although dissonants are not avoided, for the most part the lines are conservative (see ex. 2.1).

The second piece, titled "Canon," features pentachords and shows more rhythmic imagination, especially with the opening quintuplet motif. However, the slow tempo of quarter-note = 54 and the long duration of the B^2 might make the line seem stagnate, although one can imagine Fine performing it with much bravura. The canon is inverted, and in the second measure a free bass line adds dissonance and movement (see ex. 2.2).

The most interesting piece, "Scherzando," returns to the energetic motifs of her earlier music. The piece is non-imitative counterpoint so that the listener follows three independent lines in a context of more sophisticated rhythms and gestures. Near the end of "Scherzando," prior to a short recapitulation, Fine uses trills and polyrhythms to create energy and interest (see ex. 2.3).

Example 2.2. Inverted canon, pentachord, and accompanying line in "Canon," the second piece of *Four Polyphonic Pieces for Piano* (1931–32).

Example 2.3. Energy and interest in "Scherzando" from *Four Polyphonic Pieces for Piano* (1931–32).

The last piece is a Vivace two-voice invention. Fine had absorbed her counterpoint lessons. The beginning head is well shaped, and the subject is designed to develop momentum. An active countersubject helps to maintain energy. (See ex. 2.4.)

The Yaddo Festival was important because it must have given Fine a sense of being a vital part of American music. Copland organized the festival with the intention of showing the broad spectrum of American music.[25] Compositions by Ives, Sessions, Chávez, Harris, Piston, Revueltas, Rieger, Blitzstein, Thomson, and Copland were on the program. Lesser knowns at the time, such as Oscar Levant,[26] Henry Brant, Israel Citkowitz, Nicolai Berezowsky, Louis Gruenberg, Paul Bowles, and Vivian Fine, were also heard. The critics Arthur Berger and Paul Rosenfeld were at Yaddo.

Berger wrote about the festival in the May 3, 1932, final edition of the *Daily Mirror,* and Rosenfeld reviewed the events in his article "Epilogue: The Land Awaits."[27] He was not impressed with Fine's music: "the next number, four polyphonic pieces by Vivian Fine, was irritating. Three of the pieces were extremely amateurish, one was clever and slight, and none clearly justified its place on the program."[28] One wonders what was irritating. Was it the dissonance or the rhythms? Probably the amateurish aspect was the counterpoint, and it would seem that the Scherzo was "the clever and slight" movement.

Alfred Meyer wrote about the Festival for *Modern Music.* He classified the music heard as successes, near-successes, experiments, misfits, and embryos. "The two embryos are Vivian Fine, with her Schoenbergian Four Polyphonic Pieces, and Henry Brant with his suite for Flute and

Example 2.4. Beginning of the fourth piece's invention in *Four Polyphonic Pieces for Piano* (1931–32).

Piano. Both are said to be about eighteen years old. Both have natural inventiveness. Both need more skill, more definiteness of purpose, more awareness of just what it is they are about."[29]

The reviews were discouraging, but they did not stop Fine from composing. Considering her age, the *Four Polyphonic Pieces for Piano* were a major accomplishment. In Marcia Citron's study, *Gender and the Musical Canon,* she discusses qualifications necessary for having a composition accepted into the musical canon. The piece must be heard publicly, published, and reviewed. Although Fine's music was not published at that time,[30] she was heard and reviewed.

The Composers' Group did not stay in existence much longer. They gave a concert on January 15, 1933, and then disbanded because Copland was leaving for Mexico. Although Fine was definitely part of the group, she never considered Copland her teacher, but rather a valuable mentor.[31]

Meanwhile she was working on another project, *Four Songs* (1933), for mezzo soprano and string quartet.[32] These are the first songs in her catalog. Someone had given her the *Oxford Book of English Verse,* and she chose "The Lover In Winter Plaineth For The Spring" by an anonymous sixteenth-century poet, "Comfort To A Youth That Had Lost His Love" by Robert Herrick, and two poems by James Joyce, "She Weeps Over Rahoon" and "Tilly." What is significant about the songs is the way Fine used a string quartet with the voice in a context in which each line sounds separate and independent. Pitch usage resembles her previous work, atonal and disjunct, but her contrapuntal technique is more sophisticated than in the *Four Polyphonic Pieces for Piano*.

"The Lover In Winter Plaineth For The Spring" is two-voice counterpoint; the soprano is combined with the viola's quarter-note melody, which acts somewhat as a cantus firmus against the soprano's flexible syncopated rhythms. Although the meter is 4/4, Fine phrased the viola line to create changing meters of two, three, and four. A footnote to the score states: "The slurs indicate phrasing. The first note of each phrase must be brought out slightly." Layered upon this is the soprano's winding, restless, and syncopated line that never coincides with the viola's quarter-notes, and together both lines are frequently in a dissonant relationship (see ex. 2.5). Later when teaching at Bennington, Fine said to a

Example 2.5. Rhythmic interest and two-voice counterpoint in "The Lover in Winter Plaineth for the Spring" from *Four Songs* (1933).

student: "It is more interesting if you take it [an attack] off the beat,"[33] a remark Weisshaus had once made to her, and part of this song's appeal is the utter independence of the two lines.

William Upton chose to discuss "Comfort To A Youth That Had Lost His Love" in his article "Aspects of the Modern Art-Song" published in the *Musical Quarterly*. He admired Fine's song, especially her use of rhythm:

> the rhythms are vigorous, vital, incisive. . . . The declamation is extraordinarily well handled. Could anything be more natural in its rhythmical nuance than the setting of the first phrase. . . . The rhythmic alertness and spontaneity (almost that of spoken words) is one of the outstanding excellences of the composition . . . [and] this composition is eminently successful.[34]

Three-voice counterpoint is the focus of "Comfort To A Youth That Had Lost His Love," the second song. The ensemble is voice, violin, and viola, with each line being distinctive. The violin has a *cantando* above its melody, while the viola is more active with grace notes and short staccato figures that punctuate the song. The rhythmic balance is just the opposite of the first song. Here the voice is steady while often the violin and viola perform off beat (see ex. 2.6).

Example 2.6. Three-voice counterpoint in the beginning measures of "Comfort to a Youth That Had Lost His Love" from *Four Songs* (1933).

Fine used texts by Joyce for the last two songs. She is not especially a Joyce enthusiast, but just loved these passages.[35] The string quartet is heard in the third song, "She Weeps Over Rahoon," and Fine wrote for the ensemble in an imaginative way. The voice either chants the text in a quasi recitative or sings a jagged melody. The violins' dissonant harmonic drone surrounds the text with atmosphere, much as "Rain on Rahoon falls softly," the first line of the poem, while the viola and cello have melodies that act as commentaries when the voice is chanting (see ex. 2.7). This writing illustrates how Fine's compositional technique continued to develop.

"Tilly," the last of the Joyce texts, is about a cattle man longing to go home. Fine set it for voice, two violins, and cello. This song displays contrasting textures. The cello and first violin perform a unison ostinato, a new technique for Fine's music, and later a canon at two octaves. The vocal line is again disjunct and has changing meters separate from the ostinato's 6/8 meter (see ex. 2.8). When the text, "The voice tells . . .," is sung, one hears four different textures, the vocal line, a *cantando* first violin (a contrasting melody to the voice), muted double-stops of a seventh in the second violin, and pizzicato fragments in the cello. Although the song is short, the string textures create the text's mood; the vocal line is just one voice amongst the four.

There was to be a League of Composers' Concert in February 1932, and Fine wanted to have her songs performed. She went to a board meeting and sang three of them herself. As she recalls, Copland and Lazare Saminsky were two of the people present.[36] The songs were premièred at the league's February 5 concert at the French Institute. Cowell was also interested in the songs, and published them in the 1933 edition of *New Music*. At age twenty (see fig. 2.1 for a photograph of Fine at age twenty-one), she was a published and reviewed composer. Theodore Chanler wrote for *Modern Music:* "The three songs by Vivian Fine, the most 'advanced' offering of the evening, with accompaniments scored for one, two, and four stringed instruments respectively, are elaborate and sticky. It is not against their atonality that one protests, since much effective music, no less atonal than this, has been written, but against their total absence of movement."[37] His last comment about lack of movement probably applied to "She Weeps Over Rahoon," and it seems strange that he did not recognize the truly creative aspects of the song, as Upton did when writing about them in 1938, as mentioned above.

The *Four Songs* was the last of her avant garde compositions. The Depression and its related societal changes were reflected in some avant garde composers ceasing to write altogether, such as Crawford and Varèse, or others taking a new direction toward simpler music, as Copland did in his search for an American music. Fine's response was to study composition with Roger Sessions. In 1934 he was teaching the second term at the Dalcroze School in New York,[38] and accepted Fine as a stu-

Example 2.7. Advanced string writing in "She Weeps over Rahoon" from *Four Songs* (1933).

Example 2.8. Beginning measures of "Tilly" from *Four Songs* (1933).

Figure 2.1. Vivian Fine at age twenty-one.

dent. Later he left Dalcroze, and classes were held in various places, sometimes Miriam Gideon's apartment. Sessions was not interested in Fine's
previous avant garde published compositions. Instead he had her begin
with the fundamentals of harmony.[39] Fine was Sessions's student for nine
years. Studying with him influenced the way she thought about composition and, eventually, gave her an even greater confidence in her excellent

aural skills. She became more aware of tonality and the role of consonance and dissonance. In remembering her studies with him, Fine stated:

> Roger Sessions was unbelievably generous to me in my student days. He taught me for years for practically nothing and gave his concentrated attention to the exercises and compositions I brought in. Perhaps what I learned from Sessions can be described as a greater awareness of consistent musical thought. This was part of what I perceived as his overwhelming musical intellect and knowledge. Sessions did not go in for fulsome praise. "I like it" was for him quite a compliment. However, he was much taken by the opening of a piece of mine for string quartet. He said he wished he could have written it and said I had "aural vision." This remark sustained me for many years.[40]

Like Weidig, Sessions stressed the importance of aural ability, and although he did not write his text, *Harmonic Practice,* until the late 1940s, the following statement indicates what he meant by "aural vision": "The ear of the musician, as used both in creating and in apprehending, must remain the court of last appeal; and musical theory thus remains, at the very best, a more or less adequate descriptive account of the ear's experiences."[41] In the chapter about contemporary harmonic practice he wrote:

> If he [the student] is to become musically adult he will learn to make his own choices and evolve his own generalizations to the extent that he needs them. In this connection too the supremacy of the *ear* must be stressed; he must make these choices and generalizations in terms of the ear—of the music to which he most truly responds (and if he is a composer, that which he wants to produce)—of the music which he learns to *possess* and the music which he is able to *make*.[42]

Not long after beginning studies with Sessions, Citkowitz, Fine's friend from the Young Composers' Group, was influential in introducing her to Benjamin Karp, a sculptor who had just returned to the States after studying in Paris for six-and-a-half years. Citkowitz arranged a picnic in Van Cortland Park, and in April of 1935 Fine married Karp, who was employed as an artist by the Works Progress Administration. They lived in a two-room apartment in Greenwich Village that cost $26 a month. In the summer they moved to Newfoundland, New Jersey, and were fortunate to rent a house at the cost of $125 a year, the amount of the taxes, because the owners believed that rentals should not be a money-making enterprise.[43] Fine and her husband lived there for a year. The marriage did not and has not interfered with Fine's composing. "There was no question of giving it [composing] up at that time. Never."[44] In 1995 they celebrated their sixtieth anniversary.

The beginning years of the marriage were busy ones. Fine wrote *Piece for Muted Strings (Elegiac Song)* (1937) for string quartet or string orchestra, and it is an early example of her change from an avant garde to a more consonant style. She composed it as a response to the Spanish Civil War as an elegy for the children of that war. The piece is ternary, a design that Fine had not favored in the past. Changes in motifs and mode from F♯ minor to G♭ lydian create the shape. The A section's texture is homophonic with some linear movement displaying two motifs of neighbor-tones and step-wise patterns of three and sometimes five pitches (see ex. 2.9), and the B section's three-voice contrapuntal lines created from the previous motifs and prominent use of melodic fourths and fifths emphasize tonal centers.

Prelude for String Quartet (1937), the composition that Sessions praised, is similar to the previous piece in terms of gestures, meter, tempo, and tonality, but demonstrates how Fine broke the reins of tonality. Her acute hearing was able to take a simple motif of F♯-E-C♯-D-C♯-A (see ex. 2.10) and expand it into long sinuous lines. Although the *Prelude* has an A major key signature and does end on an A major triad, tonality is not a constraint, as is evidenced by the turn to flats, which lead to the F natural ending the phrase. Consonances are prevalent, and often lines having a unison rhythm move in thirds, but changes in bowings articulate the motif differently and add to textural interest, as in the 9/8 measure of example 2.10. There are occasional triadic occurrences, such as a B♭ minor and later cadences on A♭ major, but what the listener hears is a growth of the initial idea, which is free to roam tonally. The *Prelude*'s beginning has a spaciousness that suggests a longer piece (it is a mere thirty-four measures). The slowly moving gestures created by the "Molto andante, espressivo (dotted quarter = 42)" marking are given more energy when Fine breaks the eighth-note pulse into a sixteenth-note followed by a thirty-second rest and note. The repetition of this pattern and the activity it generates become the second idea of the *Prelude*. It begins as an accompaniment figure that gradually invades all four lines to become the climax of

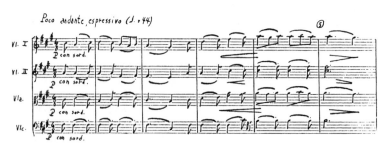

Example 2.9. Beginning measures of *Piece for Muted Strings* (1937) showing consonant motivic writing.

Example 2.10.   Beginning measures of *Prelude for String Quartet* (1937) showing roaming tonality, expansive line, and detailed bowing.

the composition in measure 18. As in her other music, there is a return to the beginning material, but subtle changes erase the sense of an exact repetition. The *Prelude* was premièred on March 26, 1939, in a League of Composers' concert. Although the *Piece for Muted Strings* and the *Prelude* work well as a pair, they were not originally intended as such.

In addition to composition lessons with Sessions, in 1937 Fine began studying piano with Abby Whiteside, a pedagogue well known for her ideas about rhythmic performance and the aural image of the music.[45] In her book, *Indispensables of Piano Playing,* Whiteside wrote: "The fun of playing and the realization of beautiful music appear only when the free play of the intricate mechanism for handling the instrument is governed by, and infused with, a controlling, encompassing rhythm."[46] Fine already had a keen rhythmic sense from her work with dancers, and she remembers that Whiteside's instruction made it easier to play the piano and less fatiguing.[47] Fine studied with her for nine years.

Fine was also active in the social concerns of the professional composer and helped to organize the American Composers' Alliance. In fact, its first meeting was held on December 19, 1937, at her home on Bleecker

Street in Greenwich Village. Copland was the president, and in the May 1938 issue of *The Dance Observer* published "A Manifesto from the American Composers' Alliance" stating the rights of composers to earn money from performance of their works.[48] Fine is an active member of the alliance and served as its vice-president from 1961 to 1965.

The years 1938–39 were busy because Fine was juggling a professional career as pianist and composer while studying. The composition lessons and work as accompanist and interpreter of modern music were Fine's way of learning about music, which she would synthesize and assimilate in her compositions. Thus performing and composing, rather than studying scores and reading what others wrote about music, was her learning style. This had been her approach since her teen years in Chicago. So it is not surprising to see some of her compositions reflecting older styles but set in her own contemporary idiom.

This is especially evident in her songs of the 1930s. Frequently Fine will set a text that interests her and then later assemble a group of songs into one collection, as in her *Four Elizabethan Songs* (1937–1941). The texts were by different poets, "Daybreak" by John Donne, "Spring's Welcome" by John Lyly, "Dirge" by Shakespeare, and "The Bargain" by Sir Philip Sidney. The songs have the same tonal orientation as the *Prelude for String Quartet* (and even similar rhythmic figures as in ex. 2.11), but

Example 2.11. Measures 4–9 showing ascending lines in "Daybreak" (1940) from *Four Elizabethan Songs*.

Example 2.12. Humor in "The Bargain" (1938) from *Four Elizabethan Songs.*

it is the piano accompaniments that are the main interest. Keyboard gestures enhance the text, such as trills and bird warbles in "Spring's Welcome" (1937) or the ascending lines in "Daybreak" (1940) when the vocal line is descending and asking that the loved one not rise (see ex. 2.11). The writing is Renaissancelike but in a contemporary setting. Fine never overwrites or uses cliches. Accompaniments are thin, and frequently there is a surprising tonal subtlety, as in measure 5 of example 2.11. Humor is especially evident in "The Bargain" (1938) with the text "There never was a better bargain driven" as shown in example 2.12. The vocal lines are well written and not complicated, and when necessary the piano provides pitch support. The songs were premièred on May 1, 1940, at the Composers Forum Laboratory in New York City. "Dirge," which was composed in 1941, was not performed at that time.

Apparently Sessions had a high regard for his student because in 1939 he dedicated the last piece from his *Pages from a Diary* to Vivian Fine and sent a copy to her with the inscription "To Vivian whom I wished lived in California."[49] Sessions was quoted as characterizing this piece as "sort of parodistic. It's a dialogue between something rather weighty and something slightly mocking."[50] This would seem to describe Fine, who has always been quite serious about her music and a bit scornful about the politic of becoming a known composer. Sessions's other three dedicatees were Milton Babbitt, Edward Cone, and Carter Harman.

By the time of her marriage Fine had developed a reputation as a dance accompanist and played for Doris Humphrey, Charles Weidman, Hanya Holm, Elizabeth Waters, Eve Gentry, and others. The jobs were demanding because there were no tape recordings, only 78 rpm records, and many choreographers preferred to have live music, so the pianist needed to be present for rehearsals, performances, and tours.[51] Often the music was transcriptions, such as Humphrey's choreography set to Bach's *Passacaglia.* Fine particularly enjoyed working with Humphrey and Weidman because they were "great dancers who had a sense of line. . . . they moved beautifully . . . and were always asking 'How does something move?' Humphrey was musical and was known for her lyrical line, and Weidman was more energetic. Both were easy to work with."[52] As accompanist, Fine had "to watch the dancer and pick up the tempo from the initial movements. Each dancer had a different quality you had to sense."[53]

Fine realized that in order to have more time for composing she needed to curtail her work as a dance accompanist. Fortunately she had opportunities to compose music for the dance. Humphrey recognized Fine's talent and wanted original music for her choreography. However, at this time modern dance was trying to remove itself from the dominance of music, and choreographers would compose their dance first, and then ask a composer to write the music.[54] This meant attending choreography sessions and counting the number of beats per movement. Naturally, these were not always even beats, and Fine would take down a rhythmic dictation of what she saw and then write music to fit.

She wrote a number of dance scores, some of which were: *Acclamations* for Charles Weidman, *Disbelieving World* and *Quest—Conversations and Affirmations* for Elizabeth Waters, and *Conviction and Evictions* for Rose Crystal.[55] But the most famous were *The Race of Life* for Doris Humphrey (1937, piano and percussion), premièred on January 23, 1938; *Opus 51* for Charles Weidman, premièred on August 5, 1938; *Tragic Exodus* (1939, piano and baritone) for Hanya Holm, premièred on February 19, 1939; and *They too are Exiles* (1939) for Holm and premièred on January 7, 1940. (Fine's *Alcestis* [1963], composed for Martha Graham, is discussed in chapter 4.)

Humphrey respected Fine's work and in 1958 wrote about their collaboration for *The Race of Life* in an article "Music for an American Dance" for the *Bulletin of the American Composers Alliance*.[56] Twenty years after the dance was created, Humphrey could write: "it was quite a score and quite an experience. She [Fine] was a true collaborator in a field, that of composing for dance, which is so different from other kinds of program music that it calls for unique qualifications."[57] The dance was based on a series of James Thurber's drawings that suggested six scenes, some of which were "The Beautiful Stranger," "Night Creatures," and "Indians."[58] Humphrey described "The Beautiful Stranger" as "no chic adolescent, but plainly bears the germ of the full-grown Thurber female, rather hard, aggressive and blowzy. To catch such conception in music was a difficult feat."[59] Mary O'Donnell, who reviewed the première of *The Race of Life*, noted how appropriate Fine's music was for the dance. "Vivian Fine's music is miraculously right for the romping nonsense it accompanies."[60] Humphrey closed her 1958 article with this appreciative statement: "in all her [Fine's] undertakings in the dance field, she has an uncanny sense of what to choose as sound and that *sine qua non* for dance composers, a complete understanding of body rhythms and dramatic timing."[61]

During the summer of 1938 Fine attended the Bennington School of Dance, working with Weidman on *Opus 51*. As before, she observed the choreography sessions, taking the counts, and then went to her small studio, which was a former chicken brooder, and composed the music. It was hard work, and sometimes it took a while before finding the underlying rhythm that would fit the dance movements. There were rehearsals everyday, too, and she found "Charles was easy to work with temperamentally. He had a crazy way of counting—he would count movements instead of beats."[62]

In 1963 Fine wrote about her experience as a dance composer and stated that the challenge of the Humphrey and Weidman choreography was "to capture the kind of comedy involved, the particular area of the human dilemma. . . . In both works I had to discover the serious musical stance from which humor could be achieved."[63] Hanya Holm's dances were based on social themes, such as the Jewish suffering under the Hitler regime, and Fine found that "the strong emotional drive in these works made musical identification comparatively easy."[64]

It was a trend during the 1930s for dance to move away from music in the sense that music was subservient. This becomes apparent when reading reviews in the *Dance Observer* and *The American Dancer*—it is rare for there to be any mention of the dance accompanist or music. O'Donnell's review of *The Race of Life* is an exception. Rudhyar even wrote about this in his article "The Companionate Marriage of Music and Dance," which appeared in the *Dance Observer,* March 1938, stating that the dancers and musicians should be on equal terms.

Although 1939 was a busy year, Fine turned her attention again to the oboe and wrote *Sonatina for Oboe and Piano* (1939) for her oboist friend, Joseph Marx. The composition won a prize in a contest sponsored by the Music Guild of Philadelphia. The *Sonatina* is in three movements (fast, slow, fast). The first movement is in a symmetrical sonata design (first theme, second theme, development, second theme, first theme); in the lyrical second movement both the oboe and piano exchange melodies and accompanimental roles; and the lively third movement features baroquelike figuration shared between both instruments. Movement one's beginning F major theme sounds like a Scarlatti sonatina, and one would expect a rather simple composition; however, the second theme exhibits Fine's penchant for doing the unexpected. The tonal center is $D^\flat$, meters change, and the piano adds energetic figures above and below the oboe's melody (see ex. 2.13). As the formal plan shows, more attention is given to the second theme. It is transposed to $G^\flat$, fragmented in the short development, and is heard in F major at the beginning of the recapitulation. When the first theme returns near the end, it is decorated with contrapuntal lines.

The second movement is a ternary song form. In the beginning the oboe has C phrygian melody, which the piano accompanies in a dissonant C

Example 2.13. First and second themes in the first movement of *Sonatina for Oboe and Piano* (1939).

major. The tonality changes for the B section, and, instead of the previous bimodality, the interest is in the contrapuntal lines that the piano adds to the oboe melody (see ex. 2.14).

The opening solo oboe material of the last movement suggests a fughetta or invention, but Fine created a binary shape of ABAB through tonal relations of F minor, G major, C minor, and G major, which eventually returns to the beginning F tonality. This is the most tonal of her music and is a striking contrast to the modernistic *Solo for Oboe* composed ten years earlier; however, Fine demonstrated that she could take simple tonal materials and manipulate them so that the listener never knows what to expect. Example 2.15 is the last A section, which has the beginning motif in C minor that when combined with the descending oboe line creates the dissonant interest found in her earlier music.

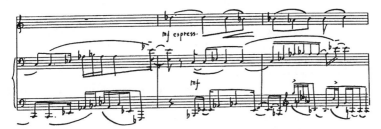

Example 2.14. Contrapuntal lines in the second movement of *Sonatina for Oboe* (1939).

Example 2.15. Motif and dissonant interest measures 21–27 of the third movement from *Sonatina for Oboe and Piano* (1939).

Composing was her love, and although Fine enjoyed writing music for dance, she began to feel that this work was too restricting. As during her early high school days she realized that her music needed more time, so she decided to stop being a dance accompanist and to devote all of her attention to her own compositions.

NOTES

1. Author's telephone interview with Fine, December 17, 1993.
2. Letter from Rudhyar to Fine dated July 1, 1931 (used with Fine's permis-

sion). The emphasis is Rudhyar's. Probably the "one you know" refers to Ruth Crawford. Apparently Rudhyar did not approve of her submission to Seeger.

3. Letter from Cowell to Fine dated August 30, 1931 (used with Fine's permission). The work that Cowell mentions in the letter is a Canon and Fugue, a piece not in Fine's active catalog.

4. Letter from Rudhyar written to Fine dated April 2. No year is given, but a penciled-in 1930 is indicated on the letter (used with Fine's permission).

5. Author's telephone interview with Fine, December 17, 1993.

6. Author's telephone interview with Fine, December 17, 1993.

7. Fine does not remember the circumstances of meeting Copland. Author's telephone interview with Fine, December 17, 1993

8. Walton was already aware of Fine's music since several years previously Crawford had told Walton about the talented young Chicago composer. In a post-card dated December 29, 1929, to Vivian, Crawford wrote: "I think of you, and speak often of you to Blanch Walton, who enjoys hearing about your work. We are counting on you." In a letter to Vivian dated July 1, 1931, Rudhyar cautioned against Vivian staying with Mrs. Walton: "But I believe this [staying with Mrs. Walton] will not be possible next winter, and, between us, it may be better so. You should be free and not too close to various quarters."(Letters used with Fine's permission.)

9. Fine remembers that Varèse and Sigetti were among the audience. Taped lecture given at the Graduate Center of CUNY, April 17, 1990.

10. Taped lecture given at the Graduate Center of CUNY, April 17, 1990.

11. Taped lecture given at the Graduate Center of CUNY, April 17, 1990.

12. Taped lecture given at the Graduate Center of CUNY, April 17, 1990.

13. This interview was conducted by Dennis Mullen for Legacy, a dance archive.

14. Author's telephone interview with Fine, December 17, 1993.

15. Arthur Berger, a member of the group, states that Copland modeled it after the French "Six." For more information see Arthur Berger, *Aaron Copland* (New York: Oxford University Press, 1953), 21.

16. Author's telephone interview with Fine, December 17, 1993.

17. Berger, *Aaron Copland,* 21.

18. Brant contributed this information for Aaron Copland's and Vivian Perlis's *Copland* (New York: St Martin's/Marek, 1984), 202–3.

19. Author's telephone interview with Fine, April 29, 1994.

20. Author's telephone interview with Fine, December 17, 1993.

21. Author's telephone interview with Fine, December 17, 1993.

22. Author's telephone interview with Fine, December 17, 1993

23. For more information about the Yaddo Festivals, see Rudy Schackelford, "The Yaddo Festivals of American Music, 1932–1952," *Perspectives of New Music,* Fall/Winter 1978, 92–125.

24. For a detailed analysis of the *Four Polyphonic Pieces* see Leslie Jones, "The Solo Piano Music of Vivian Fine," an unpublished doctor of musical arts thesis, The College-Conservatory of Music of the University of Cincinnati, 1994, 33–62. Jones does an exhaustive study, suggesting that the *Four Polyphonic*

Pieces was highly influenced by Ruth Crawford's and Scriabin's music in Fine's use of such aspects as intervals, trills, and rhythmic patterns. Many examples illustrate evidence of highly organized pitch material and contrapuntal techniques. However, in interviews with the author about use of method or favored intervals, Fine always stated she avoided any such use. It would seem that many of the compositional choices that Fine made in the *Four Polyphonic Pieces* were due to her excellent ear—she heard the ultra-modern style—rather than a conscious and labored effort to reproduce the style. In an interview with Jones quoted on page 79, Fine reinforced this lack of system. I interpret Fine's "intuitive" in the following quote as also meaning a reliance upon her acute sense of hearing:

> So much of what I had done [compositionally] up to that point [studying with Sessions] was instinctive and intuitive. This was possible for me, without being a part of any system. I went from being so entirely intuitive, almost entirely that, and you can only go so far on that. I think I developed what's called "craft." There's something in the early compositions that's very intriguing because they are so entirely intuitive. They're not without an intellectual content, but it was something I found for myself.

25. For more information about the Yaddo Festivals and the Young Composers' Group see Aaron Copland and Vivian Perlis, *Copland,* 192–94, 201–3, and 205. Pictures of the first Yaddo Festival are on 202–3. Fine is included in one of them. Marjorie Peabody Waite gives an interesting history of the Yaddo property in her book, *Yaddo: Yesterday and Today* (Saratoga Springs, N.Y.: Argus Press, 1933). Waite does not mention the festivals.

26. Apparently Levant did not enjoy being at the festival and left after performing his jazz Sonatina. He described this in his *A Smattering of Ignorance* (New York: Garden City Publishing Co, 1942), 222–26.

27. The review is included in Paul Rosenfeld, *The Discoveries of a Music Critic* (New York: Vienna House, 1972), 349–60.

28. Rosenfeld, *The Discoveries of a Music Critic,* 356.

29. Alfred H. Meyer, "Yaddo—A May Festival," *Modern Music* 10 (May-June 1932):176.

30. The *Four Polyphonic Pieces for Piano* were copyrighted in 1961 by the ACA Facsimile Edition and later made available through Fine's personal press, Catamount.

31. Author's telephone interview with Fine, December 18, 1993.

32. Stacy Ann Simons studied the *Four Songs* in her extended paper, "Vivian Fine, Netty Simons, and Nancy Van de Vate: A Singer's Look at Three American Composers" in partial fulfillment for the degree of doctor of musical arts, University of Illinois at Urbana-Champaign, 1990. Simons also performed them in recital, and her paper examines the songs from a performance aspect.

33. Fine made this comment during an interview, "Vivian Fine: A Radio Program Produced for the International League of Women Composers," produced by Ev Grimes.

34. William Upton, "Aspects of the Modern Art-Song," *The Musical Quarterly,* January 1938, 11–30. The other songs discussed in this article were "Strings in the Earth and Air" by Israel Citkowitz and Carl Ruggles's "Toys."

35. At this time she did not consider getting permission to use the texts. Her concern was to write the music.

36. Author's telephone interview with Fine, March 18, 1994.

37. Theodore Chanler, "All-American," *Modern Music, March*/April 1933, 160–62. There was also a review in the *New York Times,* February 6, 1933, stating, "Miss Fine's songs, alas, accompanied a vocal line occasionally interesting with accompaniments of mournful sterility."

38. Andrea Olmstead, *Roger Sessions and His Music* (Ann Arbor, Mich.: UMI Research Press, 1985), 67.

39. Author's telephone interview with Fine, August 25, 1994.

40. Olmstead, *Roger Sessions and His Music,* 96. In an August 25, 1994, telephone interview, Fine stated that she paid five dollars a month for weekly private lessons.

41. Roger Sessions, *Harmonic Practice* (New York: Harcourt, Brace and World, 1951), xix.

42. Sessions, *Harmonic Practice,* 384-85.

43. Author's telephone interview with Fine, March 11, 1994.

44. Author's telephone interview with Fine, April 8, 1994.

45. Whiteside wrote two books about piano technique: *Indispensables of Piano Playing* (New York: Coleman-Ross, 1955) and *Mastering the Chopin Etudes and Other Essays* (New York: Charles Scribner's Sons, 1969). She was so respected as a teacher that a group of musicians, many of whom were her former students, established the Abby Whiteside Foundation. Robert Helps was one such student, and the brochure that accompanies his recording, "New Music for the Piano" (CRI SD 288), contains a brief biography about Whiteside and a discussion of her theories about technique and performance. Fine's piece, *Sinfonia and Fugato,* is included in the recording. Joan Meggett's book, *Keyboard Music by Women Composers: A Catalog and Bibliography,* published by Greenwood Press in 1981, has some wrong information about Fine's piano teachers. Meggett states that Fine was a student of Boulanger. This is not true.

46. Whiteside, *Indispensables of Piano Playing,* 7.

47. Author's telephone interview with Fine, August 25, 1994.

48. The Manifesto listed the following names: Aaron Copland (chairman), Roy Harris, Douglas Moore, Wallingford Riegger, Elie Siegmeister, Bernard Wagenaar, Marion Bauer, Goddard Lieberson, Quincy Porter, Roger Sessions, and Virgil Thomson. Fine's name was not included.

49. Author's telephone interview with Fine, August 25, 1994.

50. Olmstead, *Roger Sessions and His Music,* 74.

51. Siegel describes these dance tours in *Days on Earth: The Dance of Doris Humphrey* (New Haven, Conn.: Yale University Press, 1987). See chapter 8, "On the Road, 1936–39," 166–84.

52. Mullen interview, see note 13 above. For more information about Humphrey, see Siegel, *Days on Earth. The Race of Life* is described on 166–84, although there is no mention of Fine's music.

53. Mullen interview, see note 13 above.

54. For a synopsis of the work of Graham, Humphrey, Weidman, and others during the 1930s see chapter 8, "Truly Modern," in Susan Au, *Ballet and Modern Dance* (London: Thames and Hudson, 1988), 119–31.

55. Mullen interview, see note 13 above.

56. Doris Humphrey, "Music for an American Dance," *Bulletin of the American Composers Alliance* 8, no.1 (1958): 4–5. Wallingford Riegger also wrote an article about Fine's music, which precedes Humphrey's.

57. Humphrey, "Music for an American Dance," 4.

58. For a photograph of Doris Humphrey, Charles Weidman, and José Limon in the *Race of Life,* see Siegel, *Days on Earth,* 168.

59. Humphrey, "Music for an American Dance," 5.

60. Mary O'Donnell, "Doris Humphrey-Charles Weidman," *The Dance Observer,* March 1938, 38.

61. Humphrey, "Music for an American Dance," 5. Later, on April 27, 1956, Humphrey revived *The Race of Life* and presented it at Juilliard Dance Theater. Fine was able to make an orchestral version of the original music, which was for piano and flexatone. Frederick Prausnitz conducted. Then Fine adapted the orchestral version for her *Ma's in Orbit* (1987) and parts of the *Memoirs of Uliana Rooney* (1994).

62. Author's telephone interview with Fine, March 18, 1994.

63. Vivian Fine, "Composer/Choreographer," *Dance Perspectives* 16 (1963): 9.

64. Fine, "Composer/Choreographer," 10.

Chapter 3

The Changing Voice

The early 1940s was a time of upset for the country, and Fine found herself going through changes.[1] Her contacts with other modern composers had dwindled since the Young Composers Group had disbanded, and although she was withdrawing from the demands of a dance composer/accompanist, working with such imaginative artists as Humphrey, Weidman, and Holm had been stimulating for Fine's creative work.

Now she found herself feeling alone as a composer, and she struggled with some personal conflicts. Crawford, her mentor, had given up composing altogether and was researching folk music. Fine was influenced "to feel that I needed an academic education."[2] Her lessons with Sessions were going well, but she was searching for her own path and voice. Studying with him meant changing to a more conservative tonal orientation. Of course this was not unique to Fine, since modernism had been replaced by much simpler styles, such as Copland adopted, but it felt like she was compromising her compositional voice. Eventually she would come to the point at which "the lessons were in my way."[3] Earlier, Weisshaus had cautioned Fine: "You do not need anybody's style, anybody's direction, . . . you are talented enough, strong enough, but only if you search for material, solution within yourself, and not in the external world, for what you do now and intend to do in the near future."[4]

Also, there was another tug—should she have followed the path of a traditional concert pianist? This was what her mother desired. Madame Herz had seen this possibility, and Abby Whiteside, with whom Fine was still studying, recognized the potential of Fine's keyboard talent. The repertoire was classical. In retrospect Fine considered this classical direction "a mistake. What I did best was to play contemporary music."[5] Although experiencing conflicts, Fine never gave up. In her words, "I had a fixed need to be involved with music and composing."[6] This is apparent in the number of pieces she wrote and premièred during this decade.

By April 1940, her work with Hanya Holm, "They Too Are Exiles" and "Tragic Exodus," was completed, so Fine had more time to devote to her own compositions. She turned her attention to the piano, the instrument of her youth, and wrote the *Five Preludes* (1939–41) and *Suite in E♭* (1940). These are virtuostic and reflect her study with Whiteside.

The five preludes are short, most one page each, highly technical, and more like etudes than preludes. All, except the last, begin tonal and end tonal with many chromatic explorations in between, a procedure Wallingford Riegger later described as "tempered atonality."[7] Each has a distinctive texture generated by one or two musical ideas, a trait that Sessions encouraged. Compared to the *Four Polyphonic Pieces for Piano,* written ten years earlier, Fine's compositional technique has become dramatic and terse, due, perhaps, to more command over a restricted use of ideas and more freedom of expression through her work with dancers. In her study, "The Solo Piano Music of Vivian Fine," Leslie Jones states: "Although the tonality of the piece [the First Prelude] is continually questionable, one feels a sense of cohesiveness and a less harsh dissonant quality than the solo piano work from her first style period (*Four Polyphonic Pieces*)."[8] For example, Prelude I uses two ideas (fluctuating thirds and a chromatic line, as stated in measure 1 of ex. 3.1) that are developed into figures having a momentum that lasts until the ending cadence.

Prelude II begins with an E♭ melody accompanied by thirds and, at times, a lower countermelody (see ex. 3.2). Through a careful use of changing meters Fine shaped asymmetrical phrases that create an unpredictable ebb and flow, and although the prelude begins and ends in E♭, the sense of tonality constantly shifts, much like the phrases themselves.

Fine's work with dancers is apparent in Prelude III (1939), which, like Prelude I, has two ideas, an arched anacrusis gesture and small scaler figures. The lines twist and turn, and the marking "Allegretto, un poco rubato" permits emphasis on the pirouetting figures (see ex. 3.3). Nowhere is there a clear tonal center until the end, which is an unexpected cadence on A♭ major.

Prelude IV (1940) reuses gestures from previous preludes. Its anacrusis figure, heard in measure 1, resembles the beginning of Prelude III; however, the gesture is developed in differing registers and contexts,

Example 3.1. Beginning measures showing fluctuating thirds and chromatic line as the two ideas of Prelude I from *Five Preludes for Piano* (1939–41).

Example 3.2. Measures 1–5 of Prelude II from *Five Preludes for Piano* (1939–41) showing tonal beginning, changing meters, and fluctuating tonality.

Example 3.3. Dancelike shapes in the beginning of Prelude III from *Five Preludes for Piano* (1939–41).

which gives it a hesitant and fluctuating character. The repeated conjunct motif written as two thirds and a fifth in measure three of example 3.4 is reminiscent of the thirds in Prelude I.

Prelude V (1941) is a brilliant perpetuum mobile line created by alternating and contrasting attacks between the right and left hands (see ex. 3.5). Occasionally the patterning is altered and in several instances a glissando is added, the first time Fine had used any such effect in her keyboard writing. This prelude adds a virtuostic closing to the set. The preludes were not premièred until 1962, twenty years after they were composed, but Fine remarked that since then her *Five Preludes* is "still played, and they are good!"[9]

While Fine was writing the *Five Preludes* she was also composing

Example 3.4. Beginning measures of Prelude IV from *Five Preludes for Piano* (1939–41) showing anacrusis figure and conjunct tonal pattern.

Example 3.5. Alternating and contrasting attacks in Prelude V from *Five Preludes for Piano* (1939–41).

Suite in E flat (1940), a more conservative collection because the *Suite* is patterned after the baroque dance suite with a prelude, sarabande, gavotte, air, and gigue.[10] However, like the *Preludes,* the *Suite* has a restricted use of one or two musical ideas, which are constantly playing with the listener's expectation. Each piece begins and ends tonally in E♭ (the Air is in C minor) and has the typical baroque figurations and required dance rhythms, but the *Suite* is definitely Fine's fun with tonality and style. For example, the prelude begins with a rather mundane figured motif in E♭, which by measure 14 is heard in a dissonant context made all the more apparent by the trills (see ex. 3.6). Other movements have tonal shifts that can be heard as contemporary-baroque fun, such as the beginning of "Gigue" (see ex. 3.7).

Three Pieces for Violin and Piano, composed the same year, has ideas similar to the *Preludes* and *Suite.* Patterned with figures that create a motor rhythm, each piece generates an energy that is shared equally by the

Example 3.6. Dissonant context of beginning motif in "Prelude" from *Suite in E flat* (1940).

Example 3.7. Tonal shift in "Gigue" from *Suite in E flat* (1940).

violin and piano.[11] Fine has an innate sense for how to direct this energy, for each piece seems to be just the right amount of time. Never does she overwrite or repeat material unnecessarily. The first piece is through-composed in the style of a baroque prelude. It begins tonally, but by measure 2 the piano adds Fine's distinctive dotted rhythmic gestures and dissonant vertical structures (see ex. 3.8). The second piece is slower and melodic, often being three-voice counterpoint due to melodies woven into the piano figuration. The last piece is a humorous gigue that at one point has the marking "misterioso" and "with exaggerated expression and rubato."

Fine earned some income by teaching piano, and, not surprisingly, used this occasion to complete a collection of children's pieces, *Music for Study* (1935–41). There are seven in the collection, and each piece is a beautiful little composition that stresses some aspect of technique, such as trills, within the context of a complete composition that is aesthetically pleasing. Some of the titles are "The Small Sad Sparrow," "Corn Song," and "Irish Lament (for the famine of 1845)."[12]

Naturally the war years were difficult, and Fine expressed her feelings in two song collections. The first consists of two songs, "Epigram" and "Epitaph: upon the death of Sir Albert Morton's Wife," on texts by Sir William Jones (1746–1794) and Henry Wotton (1568–1639). "Epigram" is a parent's hope that a baby will live, and "Epitaph" is a statement about a wife who died not long after her husband's death. They are for contralto and piano, and Fine is careful to make the text audible. She wrote the second collection, "Songs of Our Times" (1943),[13] for a concert that Lazare

Example 3.8. Beginning measures of the first piece of *Three Pieces for Violin and Piano* (1940).

Saminksy produced at the Temple Emmanuel to support the Russian/ American efforts in the war. The two songs, "Stabat Mater" and "And what did she get, the soldier's wife," are about a woman's sorrow during the time of war. The first uses a Polish text by Josef Wittlin and the second by Bertolt Brecht is in German. They are translated into English by Joy Davidman, and Fine includes both the original and English texts so that the singer may choose which language she prefers.

The Karps (Fine's married name) were also involved in assisting Louis Rapkine (1904–1948), a renowned scientist, in rescuing other French scientists from their Nazi-occupied country. Rapkine was a distant cousin of Ben's and had been a close friend when Ben was an art student in Paris. In 1988 Vivian and Ben were responsible for assembling a volume of essays on the occasion of the fortieth anniversary of Rapkine's death.[14]

The years 1942 and 1943 were busy for Fine. Her *Sonatina for Oboe and Piano* (1939) premièred in Buenos Aires on September 7, 1942. In 1943 she gave birth to their first daughter, Margaret. Motherhood was demanding, and Fine was finding it difficult to find time for composing. Fortunately Bathsheva de Rothschild, who was living in Manhattan at the time and studying at Columbia University,[15] understood and wanting to support Fine's artistry, paid for part-time help so that Fine could have several hours free each day for her music. Bathsheva's patronage made it possible for Fine to continue.

She began an important project—writing a large work, *Concertante for Piano and Orchestra* (1943). This was not commissioned (it would be 1956 when Fine was paid to write music), and there was not a scheduled première. Fine just wanted the challenge of writing for orchestra. She chose orchestral scoring of two flutes, two oboes, two clarinets in B^b, two bassoons, two horns in F, two trumpets in B^b, timpani, and standard strings. She wrote part of the score and brought it to a lesson with Sessions. Fine recalls: "He admired it very much and said extravagant things, such as 'It is much better than Bloch's *Concerto Grosso*.' He [Sessions] had studied with Bloch."[16] It was not long before Fine realized that she did not want to be a student anymore, at which time Sessions said: "Now we are colleagues."[17]

However, Fine did need some orchestration lessons. George Szell was teaching a course in orchestration at the Mannes School, and Fine attended for a semester. Her procedure at that time was to write the *Concertante* in piano score and then orchestrate it. She did not feel totally confident about these skills because she never had the opportunity to hear any of her previous pieces for orchestra (probably written during her teens and not included in her catalog). She showed her score to Szell, who said the orchestration was quite good and did not find much to criticize.[18]

The Concertante for Piano and Orchestra is in two movements, "Andante con moto (quarter-note = circa 54)" and "Allegro risoluto (quarter-note = circa 100)." The first movement follows the neoclassic concerto grosso procedures contrasting the piano against the orchestra; however, the piano is the leader in terms of its tonal freedom and the importance of material. Also, Fine tended to use the orchestra as separate choirs of strings, woodwinds, and brass, with only occasional tutti, perhaps because she was experimenting with orchestral colors. The orchestra begins with a short fanfarelike gesture that states an F major tonality. The piano replies with an unrelated five-measure phrase, also in F major, containing two ideas that will be important later in the movement—the beginning four-note descending figure and the ending rhythmic pattern of dotted sixteenth, thirty-second-, eighth-, and quarter-notes (see ex. 3.9). Structurally the *Concertante* presents an exposition (measures 1–37), development (measures 38–90), and recapitulation (measures 91–131), but, as has been Fine's procedure in the past, little material is direct repetition and each section contains unexpected tonal wanderings and elaborations upon beginning materials. Because the piano is the most adventuresome, it is the leader, and the orchestra tends to follow along. For example, at the beginning of the development, the piano states a version of the orchestra's beginning material and gradually changes it into the piano's initial expressive passage (see ex. 3.10). Soon there are superimpositions of both ideas by the piano and orchestra, such as the flute's and strings' augmentation of the piano's original four-note descending figure while the piano has figuration generated by its beginning four notes. And, in the recapitulation, the orchestra presents the piano's beginning entrance, not that the piano yields to the orchestra as a second theme succumbs to the original tonality, but more as an attempt to make the orchestra sound like the piano.

The second movement is a vigorous rondo in which the pairing of the orchestra and piano as partners becomes the A section, with the B section

Example 3.9. Beginning measures of *Concertante for Piano and Orchestra* (1943).

Example 3.10. A section of the development from *Concertante for Piano and Orchestra* (1943).

featuring the piano as a soloist with orchestral comments. The C section is developmental. The *Concertante*'s energy and virtuosity are characteristic of Fine's piano compositions and an indication of her keyboard skills and exuberance. The motion is inherent in the materials themselves, and Fine always seems to know when to end a composition. The *Concertante* was recorded by the Japan Philharmonic Orchestra, Akeo Watanabe, conductor, and Reiko Honsho, pianist (CRI 135), and in 1995 it was released on a compact disc, "American Masters: Vivian Fine" (CRI CD 692).

From 1945 to 1948 Fine was an adjunct professor at New York University. She taught piano, with the majority of the students being music

education majors. It would be almost twenty years before she was hired
to teach composition.

Meanwhile she was always busy with a composition project, and once
again wrote for oboe, this time *Capriccio for Oboe and String Trio*
(1946). She had heard Mozart's *Quartet in F major for oboe, violin, viola, and cello* and decided to try that instrumentation. The *Capriccio*
marks a new stage in Fine's writing—her music is more freely dissonant,
key signatures disappear, and tonal references are rare (see ex. 3.11). As
a result she stresses melodic line, the talent that was so apparent in her
early music. This may be one reason why the *Capriccio* is much longer.
Rather than a collection of short movements, it is divided into several sections, but the piece is designed as one long movement. Each instrument
has prominent melodies, sometimes solo and sometimes accompanied,
some of which Fine sets as canons. Trilled single lines are another feature not heard in Fine's music for a long time, and she uses trills as material for the second section of the *Capriccio*.

Early in her life as a composer, Fine learned that a piece really was not
completed until it was performed, so she was in the habit of looking for opportunities to present her music. There were two occasions in 1946: Orrea
Pernel, violinist, and Beveridge Webster, pianist, premièred *Three Pieces
for Violin and Piano* on April 16 at the Forum Group of the I.S.C.M., and
she performed *Suite in E Flat* at Temple University on November 1.

However, in 1947 she composed a piece that has never been performed, *Chaconne* for piano, her first experiment with serialism. *Chaconne* is a large work with fifteen variations over a serial chaconne theme;
however, each variation is in a two-voice texture and only the theme is
serial while the upper voice seems to be freely composed. It appears that
Fine considered this work to be a study, and maybe that is why it was
never performed.[19]

Fine's next project, *The Great Wall of China* for soprano, flute, violin,
cello, and piano (1947), is an impressive composition in which she shed

Example 3.11. The beginning measures of *Capriccio for Oboe and String Trio*
(1946).

any attempt to write tonally. This is Vivian Fine at her best, free to write what she hears. The inspiration for the song came while reading Franz Kafka's *The Great Wall of China*. Fine selected passages that attracted her interest and divided the song into four untitled movements. Then she chose soprano, flute, violin, cello, and piano as the timbres that would realize her ideas. Looking at Fine's catalog it is possible to appreciate *The Great Wall of China* as an outgrowth of some of her earlier works, such as the *Solo for Oboe,* the *Four Pieces for Two Flutes,* and the *Four Elizabethan Songs.* Also, *The Great Wall of China* is experimental and forward looking in the way she involved the ensemble in portraying the text. Only the third movement uses the full ensemble; Fine never feels compelled to have everyone playing all of the time. The soprano's text is syllabic and declamatory but set in the twisting modernistic line of her earlier music. At times she narrates with a spoken line but never is the text distorted. Fine does not use *sprechstimme* or any extended vocal techniques. Rather it is the total texture that conveys meaning. For example, in the first movement, which is for singer and flute, the flute's line, which is generally above the soprano's, portrays the emotional feeling while the singer describes the action. In example 3.12 the preceding text describes small children being required to build a wall out of pebbles. The flute line in this excerpt characterizes the teacher's wrath, and the soprano doubles the flute at an octave below for "ran full tilt against the wall" to emphasize the ascending major seventh that depicts the scene.

The second movement is about the endless frustration of trying to escape from the inner chambers of the imperial palace. Fine adds the cello so that the text is portrayed by three lines, with the singer as the middle voice. Figuration with an occasional flute or cello countermelody accompanies the singer and adds to the urgency. The text is divided into three stanzas, each preceded by an introduction and ended with an interlude. Each time this happens the music is somewhat similar, but never identical. Fine is careful to vary her material, as is evident in example 3.13, which illustrates the continually varied cello figuration and flute countermelody.

As the movements progress, the listener begins to realize that Fine's music is also building a wall. The third movement adds the piano, and, again, the voice is in the middle of a five-voice texture that often sounds like a

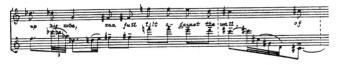

Example 3.12. Text and emotional feeling in the first movement of *The Great Wall of China* (1947).

Example 3.13. Cello figuration and flute countermelody in the second movement of *The Great Wall of China* (1947).

wall. The text relates the uncertainty about which dynasty is reigning and confusion about history and reality. Fine portrays this confusion in several ways. Sometimes the soprano just speaks as a narrator and at other times she sings, frequently in a low register, which contributes to the text's darkness and gloom. An even more important aspect is that this movement contains elements of the previous two. The thirty-second double dotted eighthnote figure heard in example 3.13 becomes part of an introductory motif that signals the beginning of each stanza in the third movement. For the third stanza, which is the most complex, Fine took the cello figuration at the beginning of movement two, augmented it for the left-hand part of the piano, used a diminuted version for the right hand, which is also doubled by the flute, and composed new vocal material, which is doubled at the octave below by the cello (see ex. 3.14). The wall image is readily apparent, and this is the first time she constructed her music to be referential.

The fourth movement contains further complexities, including serial procedures. The cello introduces a twelve-tone row [C♯-D-C-E♭-E-G♯-F-G-B-A♯-A-F♯] in measures 2–4 and this becomes the basis for much of the counterpoint. The row is not transposed, but Fine does use a retrograde for the vocal line at section D and permits freedoms, such as repeating pitches out of order and repeating material from previous movements. The flute line in example 3.15 at rehearsal letter G is the beginning melody from movement one; the cello's cantabile melody is from movement three; and the piano's *sotto voce* is reminiscent of its low thirds in movement three.

During 1948 Fine premièred two compositions, *Capriccio for Oboe and String Trio* (1946) on April 17 at the I.S.C.M. Forum Group and *The Great Wall of China* (1947) in May in an Alice Ditson Fund Concert. As was her

Example 3.14. Walls of material in movement three of *The Great Wall of China* (1947).

custom, she liked to make her music public and was pleased that *The Great Wall of China* was published that same year in *New Music*. She also taught a class, "Materials of Music," at Juilliard for one semester. The year of 1948 marked several changes in Fine's life. Her second daughter, Nina, was born and the family moved to Montclair, New Jersey, not an easy move because the location isolated her from the musical life of New York City.

Another move happened in 1951 when Ben took a faculty position in the art department of the New York State University at New Paltz. Again, New Paltz felt like isolation, but as always, Fine continued composing, this time *Divertimento for Violoncello and Percussion* (1951). Fine chose cello and percussion (cymbal, tambourine, wood blocks, snare drum, and timpani), an unusual combination in her catalog. The *Divertimento* di-

Example 3.15. Reuse of previous material at letter G in movement four of *The Great Wall of China* (1947).

vides into four sections forming a loose A (measures 1–30), B (measures 31–67), B (measures 68–108), A (measures 109–35) pattern. The A material is an active cello melody displaying Fine's penchant for writing a well–articulated but tonally free line. The percussion is heard as an accompaniment (see ex. 3.16). The B sections place more emphasis on the percussion, sometimes creating duets between the ensemble and cello or isolating individual colors, such as timpani and cello (see ex. 3.17).

Fine's reuse of material is always clever, and like in her earlier music, avoids exact repetition. For example, the cello's beginning pitches of $C^{\#}4$-B^3 become a playful four-measure elaboration during measures 110–14 delaying the return of the original melody, which has a new percussion accompaniment.

Fine took advantage of an opportunity to teach composition at the State University of Potsdam during the summer of 1951. She and Stanley Kunitz, a poet, designed a class that introduced composition to a variety of students, most of whom were elementary and high school teachers. Fine enjoyed the experience, which, although she did not realize it, was a good preparation for her future work at Bennington.

Meanwhile Fine was occupied with a large piece, *Variations for Piano*

Example 3.16. Cello melody accompanied by percussion in measures 4–6 of *Divertimento for Violoncello and Percussion* (1951).

Example 3.17. Isolated timbres of cello and timpani in measures 83–89 in the B section of *Divertimento for Violoncello and Percussion* (1951).

(1952). Later she extracted the *Sinfonia* and *Fugato* from the *Variations* to be included in *New Music for the Piano,* a Lawson-Gould Publication honoring Abby Whiteside, which Robert Helps recorded for RCA Victor and was later reissued by Composers Recordings Inc. (CRI SD 288).[20] Fine's *Sinfonia* is sonorous, angular, and somber, having an etudelike quality featuring contrary motion, often in sixths, that creates an interesting use of tight and spacious registers. Dotted rhythmic patterns contribute a heaviness and seriousness (see ex. 3.18).[21]

The *Fugato* is Fine's first use of traditional counterpoint for a complete piece, and a casual listener might mistake it for one of the fugues from Hindemith's *Ludus tonalis.* The *Fugato* is in three voices with two subjects. The first begins with a traditional hammerhead figure followed by

Example 3.18. Beginning measures of *Sinfonia* (1952) showing contrary motion. (Copyright © 1963 by the Lawson-Gould Music Publishers, Inc.; used by permission.)

large leaps, characteristics that allow the listener to follow the fugal procedure (see ex. 3.19). Its answer is accompanied by a countersubject. The second subject is more active rhythmically and has its own exposition that presents a clear tonal center of C. The reminder of the *Fugato* is episodes using the heads of each subject until the ending, which is a complete statement of the first subject.

Fine's next composition, *Sonata for Violin and Piano* (1952), is a further exploration of the energy and drive that are heard in the *Concertante* and *Sinfonia* and *Fugato*. This three-movement work is the first time she had used the term "sonata," and it is more in the spirit of contrast and reuse than the development and process of the traditional form. Fine's *Sonata* does not exhibit a hierarchy: the violin and piano are equal partners, and although each state differing material at the beginning of the three movements (one hears a violin theme followed by a piano theme), sometimes the materials are used in canon or exchanged as in measure 93 of the first movement in which the violin has material the piano stated earlier in measure 16. The *Sonata*'s tonal freedom, rhythmic flexibility, and jagged melodic contour are a return to Fine's innate talent expressed in the early works, such as *Solo for Oboe*. What has changed is her ability to work on a larger scale; the *Sonata* is fifteen minutes long. The first movement is an ABAB shape created by the beginning "Energico, confuoco (ca eighth-note = 144)" constituting the A section, which changes in measure 27 to a

Example 3.19. First subject of *Fugato* (1952). (Copyright © 1963 by the Lawson-Gould Music Publishers, Inc.; used by permission.)

contrasting "delicato, cantabile" two-voice canon between the violin and the piano's lower registers. A recapitulation happens in measure 81, almost midpoint of this 155-measure movement, producing an ABAB shape. A development section as such is not heard, because Fine often reuses material making changes in rhythm, altering melodic patterns, or exchanging music between the instruments. However, something new to Fine's writing occurs in measures 66–69—she repeats a measure four times in order to create tension in a passage that is leading to the recapitulation. When describing her compositional style, Fine stated: "It took me a long time before I would repeat something exactly."[22]

The slower second movement, "Lento (ca eighth-note = 52)" is relaxed and spacious. There is no meter, and the constantly changing rhythmic groupings (see ex. 3.20) resemble Olivier Messiaen's use of additive rhythm. Again, both instruments present contrasting material, the piano's implied minor ninth chord with its pedal root and the violin's long lyrical melody. The chordal motif becomes important because it is restated, transposed, altered, and exchanged during the movement. Again there is a midpoint recapitulation, but the movement resembles a series of variations due to the prominent repetition of the piano motif and violin melody. As is her custom, Fine disguised the repetitions, truncating and expanding the material and having several tight canons between the violin and upper piano register.

The third movement functions as a scherzo, with the violin having a solo three-measure gypsylike theme that the piano repeats with some adaptation. Fine's manipulation of material is more apparent in this movement. The sixteenth-note head of the violin melody and the piano's initial percussive eighth-note figure (see ex. 3.21) are heard frequently, sometimes in a three-voice canon as in measures 18–21, in sequences as in measures 55–57, or developed and enlarged as in measures 58–59. Due to the frequent repetitions of the beginning material, this movement as-

Example 3.20. Beginning measures of the second movement of *Sonata for Violin and Piano* (1952).

Example 3.21. Beginning of movement three of *Sonata for Violin and Piano* (1952) showing piano and violin motifs.

sumes a rondo shape of ABACA of uneven proportions with A being measures 1–34, B measures 35–43 with a tempo change to "Meno mosso," A measures 44–52 with a return to the original tempo, C measures 53–81 as a freer and more developmental section, and another return to A in measures 82–90. This last movement resembling a sonata-rondo is closer to a traditional form used in the sonata process.

Even though Fine was feeling isolated in New Paltz, she made certain that the *Sonata* was heard in New York. It was premièred on December 21, 1958, by Matthew Raimondi, violinist, and Yehudi Wyner, pianist, at the Composers' Showcase Concert.

In the summer of 1953 she experimented with a neoclassic style for *Variations for Harp,* dedicated to Joyce Rosenfield and subtitled "Remembrance of things in the past of Erik Satie."[23] The simple pandiatonic theme (see ex. 3.22) has four variations plus a finale, with the last variation being the most interesting due to its inverted form of the theme and transpositions to G♭ major and F minor, tonal references suggested by the theme's beginning motif of an ascending fifth. Fine would refer to Satie again in 1979 in a larger piece, *For a Bust of Erik Satie,* using text, singers, six instruments, and narrator.

Earlier, in 1953, Fine was honored with an important role as music director of the Bathsheva de Rothschild Foundation for Art and Sciences,

Example 3.22. Beginning measures of *Variations for Harp* (1953). (Copyright © 1965 by LYRA MUSIC CO; used by permission.)

an appointment Fine would serve until 1960. The main function of the foundation was to support Martha Graham; however, Rothschild also wanted to promote concerts of contemporary music. Fine was a personal friend, and Bathsheva also had the strong recommendation from Gregor Piatigorsky, Rothschild's brother-in-law, concerning Fine's abilities.[24] Part of Fine's function as music director was to plan concerts that the foundation supported and to recommend grant awards.

In 1956 Rothschild made it possible for Fine to receive her first commission, which was premièred in the inaugural concert of the B. de Rothschild Foundation Concert Series. Fine chose to write *A Guide to the Life Expectancy of a Rose, a Scene for soprano, tenor flute, violin, clarinet, 'cello, and harp* (1956). Naturally the commission guaranteed a performance, and Fine was in the situation of doing whatever she wanted, including selecting performers, such as Bethany Beardslee and Jacques Monod. Fine chose to use text, a compositional milieu that had been so successful for her in the past. (Recall that her two published works in *New Music* were *Four Songs* and *The Great Wall of China*.) However, her text was rather unconventional—she selected an article by S. R. Tilley from the *New York Times* garden page. Later she would use newspaper material as the idea for her opera, the *Memoirs of Uliana Rooney*.

Although the text is a straightforward discussion about the growing habits of various kinds of roses, such as floribunda, hybrid tea roses, and climbers, Fine saw an opportunity to consider the text as a metaphor for human relationships. Her previous work with dance composition, especially Doris Humphrey's *The Race of Life,* fueled Fine's imagination for considering Tilley's article about growing roses as a scene, much like a chamber opera. Fine divided the article into five sections: (1) "Longevity an interesting point on which to speculate," (2) "Some must be discarded," (3) "Replacement and survival," (4) "Ramblers and climbers," and (5) "Protection and mortality." She indicated certain props and actions for the soprano and tenor.

Martha Graham directed the première, which was May 15, 1956, at her dance studio.[25] In notes which accompany the score Fine described the staging:

In the version directed by Martha Graham for the Composers'
Forum in New York City the instrumentalists sat on one side of the
stage, the action taking place on the other side. Miss Graham dressed
the singers in formal clothes of the Edwardian period. In addition,
she used three male dancers, who set the stage with artificial rose-
bushes in pots, and who were utilized during pauses between
sections.

Fine's sense of humor and compositional talent merged to produce one
of her finest compositions and a predecessor for her future operas.
    Although *A Guide to the Life Expectancy of a Rose* is not recorded pro-
fessionally, there is a tape recording of the première, and what is immediately apparent from listening is the text's clarity. The audience's laughter
recorded on the tape confirms this fact. Fine knows how to compose for
singers so that every word is audible. There are some spoken words, sections of recitative, duets, solos, and a short spoken passage resembling
sprechstimme. Her keen sense of rhythmic flow complements the text's
natural declamation, plus her innate musical hearing allows her to write
lines that enhance the words. Fine reported that she heard the piece while
she was composing it and composed it chronologically and in full score.[26]
Since she is not bound by some predetermined order of a pitch system, she
is free to write with attention to clarity. She knows what it will sound like.
    The instrumental ensemble of flute, violin, clarinet, 'cello, and harp
provides color and texture. Sometimes vocal lines are doubled or punctuated by the ensemble. At other times the instrumental counterpoint provides a further commentary about the text, such as the twisting lines that
begin section four, "Ramblers and climbers" (see ex. 3.23, page 27 of the
score) or an ostinato that accompanies the woman's text discussing a
rosebush's healthy roots. There are several instances in which an instrument acts as a vocalist. An especially interesting example is when the
male vocalist chants a text "There are ever so many conditions that influence longevity" while accompanied by a solo pizzicato cello line that
was a melody he had sung four measures previously, creating a situation
in which he is singing against himself. *A Guide to the Life Expectancy of
a Rose* is sixteen minutes long, and the listener hears it as one complete
work. Sections are apparent by staging directions, which Fine included
in the score. For example, section three, "Replacement and survival," begins with the following action: "During this section the man remains
seated. The woman moves about freely. She does not direct her singing
to him." Short instrumental introductions set the mood, except for the last
section, which functions as a recapitulation repeating previous music
from sections one and two, which have been adjusted for text considera-
tions. Fine indicates that it is possible to perform *A Guide to the Life Expectancy of a Rose* as a concert piece.

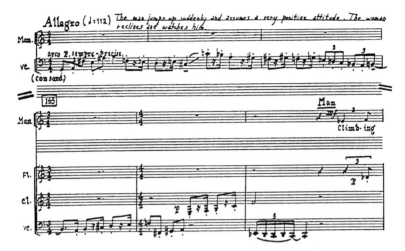

Example 3.23. Instrumental commentary in *A Guide to the Life Expectancy of a Rose* (1956).

Fine's next project was *String Quartet* (1957), a medium she had not used for twenty years since *Prelude for String Quarlet* (1937) and *Piece for Muted Strings (Elegiac Song)* (1937). The 1957 *String Quartet* is a large work of four movements totaling twenty minutes. The *Quartet* is heard as one large composition since the four movements are joined with attacas, elisions, or an abrupt cadence that links movements one and two.

With *A Guide to the Life Expectancy of a Rose* and the *Quartet* Fine seems to have advanced to a more mature level of composition. The angular lines from her early music are replaced by longer and more graceful curves. She is comfortable with large-scale designs, and although the *Quartet* has no text, the music has a dramatic quality that was such an important aspect of *A Guide*. Its humor is replaced with a seriousness and intensity that changes from movement to movement while maintaining an overall expressiveness. The first movement is a sonata design that is more structured than Fine had used in the past due to her fleeting reference to temporary tonal centers amidst an atonal environment. This was most apparent in her music of the 1940s, but by this time it had become much more powerful because the tonal references are more subtle.

Later, in 1958 Riegger would write about Fine's tendency as "atonality, tempered occasionally by key impressions."[27] An example is the first theme, which is tempered to have an F center. The beginning pitch F, the G-C-F heard from measure 3 to measure 4, and the low C in the cello at measure 6 strengthen the F reference (see ex. 3.24, measures 1–5 of the

Example 3.24. First theme in first movement of *String Quartet* (1957).

first movement). In measure 12 the theme is transposed to a C level suggesting that at least vague tonal references will be important in the *Quartet*. Adding to the temperament idea are this movement's three themes (first theme, second theme, and closing theme), which share common properties, such as a head interval of a major seventh and similar rhythmic patterns. Fine emphasizes these similarities near the end of the movement by juxtaposing references to the first theme with a complete second theme in measures 149–50 and then a bold reiteration of the first and closing themes' heads (see ex. 3.25). Included in this example is the abrupt cadence mentioned earlier linking the first and second movements. Texture also contributes to this movement's design. Transitions using fragments of the themes, repeated passages, and sudden changes in dynamics lead to important thematic statements, and the development, though a short thirty-seven measures, divides into four sections made apparent by changes in texture and dynamics.

The second movement is an "Allegro di Bravura (quarter-note = 132)" with a 9/8 meter, which is heard as a ternary dance plus coda. Fine uses the metric regularity as a backdrop for interesting manipulations of patterns, such as repetition, truncation, elongation, inversion, and occasional tonal references. Example 3.26 illustrates how the violin melody first presented in measures 8–10 is reused by the second violin in measures 35–38 with different phrasing and accompanying material. Due to the bravura tempo, ideas pass quickly, and the second movement is suddenly elided

Example 3.25. Reiteration of first and closing themes' heads at the ending of the first movement of *String Quartet* (1957).

Example 3.26. Pattern manipulation in the second movement of *String Quartet* (1957).

to the slow and dense third movement. The listener's attention is drawn to the harmonic action often created by linear action but sometimes intended as accompanying material, such as the violin drones that accompany the cello melody in example 3.27 (measures 7–8). Fine let her acute sense of hearing choose the harmonic tension of the drone since no intervallic or other scheme is determining pitch choices.

The last movement is marked "Allegretto a la danza (eighth-note = 208)" and is unusual because Fine uses a seven-measure metric pattern that becomes a theme with variations. The changing meters are marked clearly in the melody, as seen in example 3.28 (measures 1–7), which

Example 3.27. Harmonic interest in the third movement of *String Quartet* (1957).

Example 3.28. Metric theme of the fourth movement of *String Quartet* (1957).

Fine repeats with the addition of a simple counterpoint so that the listener becomes aware of its importance. Later in the movement the melodies and textures change, as in example 3.29 (measures 36–39), yet the metric scheme's thematic significance is maintained. Eventually the metric pattern is disturbed, which adds contrast to the piece. Fine is always careful to include alterations so that her music never becomes predictable. A return to a unison statement of the beginning seven-measure phrase produces a recapitulation that ends the *Quartet.*

In 1957 Fine's scores were published by the American Composers' Alliance as part of its Composers' Facsimile Edition. Then in August 1958 Riegger wrote an article, "The Music of Vivian Fine,"[28] discussing *A Guide to the Life Expectancy of a Rose* in detail and including examples of her early *Four Pieces for Two Flutes.* Riegger was impressed by Fine's orchestration of *The Race of Life,* and closed his article by quoting several earlier reviews of her work. First mentioned was William Upton's 1938 review of Fine's *Four Songs,* which praised her for "the composer's meticulous care in handling her declamation—an unfailing virtue in Miss Fine's song writing." Next, Lazar Saminsky wrote in the *Musical Courier* that "Vivian Fine is a creator of music of fine substance and outstanding mastery. . . . In her Concertante for Piano and Orchestra it is a delight to follow the novel diatonic flow. Even more impressive are her splendid songs—beautiful in emotional depth and a masterly mirroring

Example 3.29. Texture and melodic change in the metric theme of the fourth movement of *String Quartet* (1957).

of amazingly potent, fine intellect." Last, Riegger recalled Cowell's early support of Fine: "Among composers in the central part of the United States the most interesting figure is Vivian Fine. . . . Her work possesses a good form, and reveals a restless and agile talent" and Cowell's later opinion: "the inner qualities [of Fine] are the same—natural technique and a rigid lack of compromise with anything but her very best."[29]

Following Riegger's article is Doris Humphrey's "Music for An American Dance," which was discussed earlier. Fine's catalog is included, which by this time occupied two pages of a double-column listing.

NOTES

1. For more information about music in American society during this time see Barbara Zuck, *A History of Musical Americanism* (Ann Arbor, Mich.: University of Michigan Research Press, 1980), 89–101.

2. Author's telephone interview with Fine, May 20, 1994.

3. Author's telephone interview with Fine, February 23, 1995.

4. Letter from Weisshaus to Fine dated August 23, 1931 (used with Fine's permission). Weisshaus emphasized this passage in his letter by putting an extra space between every letter, thus showing the importance of his statement.

5. Author's telephone interview with Fine, March 9, 1995.

6. Author's telephone interview with Fine, March 9, 1995.

7. See the later discussion in Riegger's article, "The Music of Vivian Fine," in *The Bulletin for the American Composers Alliance*, 8/1 (58): 2–4.

8. Jones, "Solo Piano Music," 95.

9. Author's telephone interview with Fine, May 20, 1994.

10. For a detailed analysis of the *Suite in E flat* see Jones, "Solo Piano Music," 101–40.

11. Lou Harrison reviewed the première of *Three Pieces,* which occurred at the International Society for Contemporary Music's Forum Concert at Times Hall. Harrison wrote in the *New York Herald Tribune,* April 17, 1946: "Orrea

Pernel was the violinist in Vivian Fine's *Three Pieces,* which this listener found undecided in stylistic address and a bit rambunctious in workmanship, though also having a strong rhythmic feeling."

12. See Jones, "Solo Piano Music," 83–92, for a study of *Children's Suite* that includes numerous musical examples.

13. The "Songs" were not available for study.

14. Vivian Karp and Benjamin Karp, *Louis Rapkine* (North Bennington, Vt.: The Orpheus Press, 1988).

15. For more information about Bathsheva de Rothschild, see *The French Rothschilds* by Herbert R. Lottman (New York: Crown, 1995), 185, 214, 217, 234–35, 237, and 312–14.

16. Author's telephone interview with Fine, March 11, 1994.

17. Author's telephone interview with Fine, March 11, 1994.

18. Author's telephone interview with Fine, March 11, 1994.

19. Jones has studied *Chaconne* and illustrates Fine's use of serialism. See "Solo Piano Music," 147–59.

20. The Abby Whiteside Foundation, established by a group of her students, sponsored the Lawson-Gould publication and the recording. Also included in this boxed set are pieces by Ingolf Dahl, Samuel Adler, Milton Babbitt, Mel Powell, Alan Hovhaness, and others. The record liner notes by Joseph Prostakoff state that

> the biographies of the composers of these pieces . . . show that a great majority of them teach at universities throughout this country. Thus, they have a particular importance because they exert a twofold influence on the formation of musical tastes of the future. It is also interesting to note that, with few exceptions, they are close to each other in age. That makes this collection represent to some extent the music of an entire generation of composers.

21. Jones, "Solo Piano Music," discusses the *Sinfonia and Fugato* on 159–71.

22. Author's telephone interview with Fine, May 20, 1994.

23. The published version of *Variations for Harp* has an error. The date given at the end of the composition is "Summer-1963." It should be 1953. The piece was premièred April 22, 1955, at Woodstock, New York, by Joyce Rosenfield.

24. Earlier, Fine had showed Piatigorsky her *Sonatina for Oboe and Piano,* which she had arranged for cello and piano. Piatigorsky admired the work, although he never performed it.

25. Ross Parmenter writing in the *New York Times* on May 16, 1956, reviewed the concert and described how the studio was transformed into a concert area. He found that "the humor implicit in setting so unlikely a text [*A Guide to the Life Expectancy of a Rose*] was frayed." Other pieces on the concert were three scenes from Monteverdi's "Il Ritorno d'Ulisse in Patria," Sonata for 'Cello and Piano by Herman Barris, four songs by William Ames, Toccata for piano by Charles Haubiel, Prelude, Passacaglia and Finale for piano and "From the Dead Sea Scrolls" for baritone and piano by Jacob Weinberg.

26. Author's telephone interview with Fine, May 22, 1996.

27. Wallingford Riegger, "The Music of Vivian Fine," *Bulletin of the American Composers Alliance* 8, no. 1 (1958): 2–4.

28. Riegger, "The Music of Vivian Fine," 2–4.

29. Riegger, "The Music of Vivian Fine," 4.

Chapter 4

The Maturing Voice

The Rothschild concerts gave Fine a venue for performing some of her own compositions, and in 1959 her *Valedictions* (1959), a large work for SATB chorus, soprano and tenor soloists, and a small chamber orchestra of ten instruments, was premièred by Hugh Ross and the Schola Cantorum. Fine used texts by John Donne that express sadness and grief. She set these in traditional choral fashion, repeating text at times, featuring duets between the soloists, and using full chorus to create various textures. There are short instrumental sections serving as introductions and interludes, but generally, the small orchestra doubles or colors the vocal parts. Compared to *A Guide to the Life Expectancy of a Rose* and the *String Quartet, Valedictions* is a more conservative composition. It is lacking the long graceful lines and mature voice heard in these pieces. Perhaps the reason is that *Valedictions* is Fine's first SATB choral composition.

In 1960 she returned to a medium she had not composed for in twenty years. Martha Graham asked Fine to write the music for a ballet, *Alcestis.* Graham had been aware of Fine's music since the 1930s, and, of course, she knew Fine's position in the Rothschild Foundation. Graham's working procedure was much different than it had been in Fine's previous experience with choreographers. Heretofore the choreography preceded the music. With *Alcestis,* Fine wrote the music from a dramatic script written by Graham.[1] As stated on the score, Fine's intention was "an attempt to depict the dramatic and emotional qualities of the myth . . . [that] avoids descriptive or representational writing." The score is self-sufficient, and later she would quote passages, such as the opening in example 4.1, in other compositions. Fine distilled the essence of the myth into a sonic drama expressed by contrapuntal lines enhanced by imaginative orchestration and flexible rhythms to complete the composer's realization of *Alcestis.* It was premièred on April 29 and May 8 at the 54th Street Theatre.[2] Later Fine extracted sections of the ballet score to create an independent composition that is divided into the following sections: (1) Alcestis and

67

Example 4.1. Beginning of *Alcestis* (1960).

Thanatos, (2) The Revelling Hercules, (3) Battle between Hercules and Thanatos, and (4) The Dance of Triumphs and The Rescue of Alcestis. The music was recorded on CRI (CRI 145) by the Imperial Philharmonic of Tokyo, William Strickland, conductor. In 1995 it was released as a compact disc version, CD 692 in CRI's American Masters series.

In 1961 Fine assumed the duties of vice-president of the American Composers' Alliance, an organization of which she was a founding member. She served a four-year term.

During the same year she wrote *Duo for Flute and Viola* (1961) for flutist Claude Monteux (the son of distinguished French conductor Pierre Monteux) and violist Walter Trampler, who was well known for his performance of contemporary music.[3] Not surprisingly, Fine's *Duo* is virtuostic. There are no barlines or meter, and sudden changes of tempi, one of which is caused by a metric modulation, enhance its artistry. The *Duo* is an outgrowth of the *String Quartet,* as evidenced in its long arching lines and directions for changes in timbral quality, such as "explosively," "clear," "stridente," and "easy." Each instrument has a cadenza, but most interesting is the counterpoint between the two (see ex. 4.2.) There is no imitation or exchange of material, giving each instrument an independent voice. Fine does refer to the *Duo*'s beginning near the end of the piece, but the material soon changes to become a perpetuum mobile ending. The *Duo* was copyrighted by Carl Fischer in 1976 and published as a Carl Fischer Facsimile Edition. Fine does not recall the details of this publication, being quite certain that she did not submit the score.[4]

Fantasy for Cello and Piano (1962), Fine's next composition, is also a duo. She stated her intentions in the score's preface: "The idiom is a kind of musical abstract expressionism: dramatic contrasts grow out of materials stated at the outset, developed with lyrical freedom confined with a degree of composerly rigor." [5] Rarely does Fine make such a statement about her music, but this one shows she realizes that her early severe modernistic style had evolved to an abstract expressionism, allowing her complete aural freedom, which she expresses as a "fantasy," a new term in her catalog. The composition has sudden texture changes, which produce dramatic contrasts within a seamless structure. Subtle

Example 4.2. Non-imitative counterpoint in *Duo for Flute and Viola* (1961). (Copyright © 1979 by Carl Fischer; used with permission.)

dovetailing, such as elisions, join one section to another. Generally the cello and piano function as equals, sometimes exchanging material, accompanying each other, or playing in unison.

One of the most interesting aspects about *Fantasy* is the growth and development of beginning material that states four ideas: a lyric line marked "with serene intensity," a powerful melody highlighted with accents and marcatos, chordal punctuations (see ex. 4.3), and tremolo figures. These ideas are developed progressively, a feature not often found in Fine's music, and her statement about "composerly rigor" is accurate.

The composition was premièred on a concert of music by American women sponsored by the National Federation of Music Clubs on February 13, 1970, in Carnegie Recital Hall by John Thurman, cellist, and Robert Guralnick, pianist.[6] It has frequently been performed by Maxim Neuman, cellist, and Joan Stein, pianist, and still remains in their repertory.

Fine had another opportunity to write for strings when bassist Bertram

Example 4.3. Measures 9–16 of *Fantasy for Cello and Piano* (1962).

Turetzky came to Bennington in 1964. Becoming well known as a pro-
moter of extended techniques on that instrument,[7] Turetzky was eager to
play new works, and Fine took the opportunity to write a solo piece, *Melos,* her first such work since she had written her *Solo for Oboe* (1929)
and *Second Solo for Oboe* (1947). Fine uses the double bass traditionally
without any extended techniques. There are no double stops, unusual
bowings, percussive or speech sounds, and only one harmonic. Instead
she chose to have her piece be a character study. It begins traditionally
with the melodic shapes and long lines she often uses but then the emotional quality changes. Markings indicate "tranquillo," then a sudden
"espressivo" associated with dynamic fluctuations from pp to mf hap-
pening every two or three pitches, a long "più intenso" phrase is followed
by an active "con nobilità" passage (see ex. 4.4). The closing portion of
Melos is "con slennità" that is transformed into "misurato" for its final
phrase. Turetzky is such a dramatic performer that one could imagine appropriate body language associated with *Melos* that would add touches
of humor that are not foreign to Fine's music. Turetzky premièred *Melos*
on April 8, 1964, at Bennington.

The fall of 1964 brought a change in Fine's life—she was offered a
half-time position at Bennington College. Paul Boepple,[8] who was the
choral director, was retiring. Already on the faculty were Louis Calabron,
George Finckel, Gunar Schonbeck, Frank Baker, who taught voice and
knew Fine, Lionel Novack, who had joined Fine for some of the piano
accompaniments for Doris Humphrey's dances, and Henry Brant, who
was a colleague in the Young Composers' Group.

In reflecting about the position, Fine remarked that at Bennington the
philosophy was: "you teach what you are," [9] in which case, Fine had a lot
to give. In addition she realized: "they wanted a woman." [10] By this time
she was fifty-one years old,[11] an established composer and performer, and
an experienced teacher. She brought to her students the same kind of en-
thusiasms and empowering that Ruth Crawford had given her. Crawford
taught Fine to pursue "adventurous interesting music [and that compos-
ing] was the most normal thing." [12] Fine did the same for her students at

Example 4.4. Dramatic changes in *Melos* (1964).

Bennington, and the majority of her students were female. In 1975 she described this situation:

> When I first came here [Bennington], it was entirely female. That was in 1964; now [1975] it varies. My first year class consisted of . . . fourteen or fifteen women and one man. . . . We have talented women at Bennington and I hope that the feeling of composing is [a] natural thing for a woman to do, and that it will continue here. I think one of the reasons they wanted to have a woman composer on the staff was that they'd never had one here before, and I certainly think that this is very important anywhere to *have* a woman. Looking back, I realize that it was of incalculable importance that I had Ruth Crawford as a teacher and as a model in my life.[13]

She taught Music 1 (a mixture of composition and theory resembling the philosophy of comprehensive musicianship) and piano. Known for its experimental programs,[14] Bennington's music department believed that beginners should compose and perform because studying music meant equal attention to both. Students were given a concept, such as duration, and then assigned to write a short rhythmic composition using only a few pitches, such as the open strings on the cello. Fine believes that anyone can compose: "I never had a student who didn't compose something." [15] She also believes that composition cannot be taught, but students are made aware of materials.[16] Faculty performed the pieces so that students learned from the aural experience. Several composers came out of the Bennington program, such as Joan Tower and Elizabeth Swados, who wrote about her learning experience in *Listening Out Loud: Becoming a Composer.*[17]

Fine was an ideal teacher for Bennington since her career combined a strong performance background with a vigorous compositional life. In addition, since she taught composition at the State University Teachers' College at Potsdam in the early 1950s and in 1963 taught composition to dancers during the summer session of the Connecticut School of Dance, Fine was well prepared to assume her duties at Bennington. She remembers being offered the position: "My name came up. I was hesitant about being away part of the week." [18] At that time she still lived in New Paltz because her husband was teaching there, so her Bennington duties were arranged for only a few days each week. Faculty members were appreciative of Fine's piano skills, and it was not long before rehearsals and performances were scheduled on days that Fine was on campus so that she could participate. By 1969 Fine was offered a full-time position, so the family moved to Shadesbury, Vermont, and Ben commuted to New Paltz. Meanwhile they were having a house built in Hoosick Falls, New York, their residence since that time, which is a just a few miles from Bennington.

In retrospect, teaching at Bennington was a turning point. For over twenty years Fine composed, for the most part, in isolation, a strong contrast to her early days in which she participated in Madame Herz's salon concerts and corresponded with Cowell and Rudhyar. Even when she moved to New York City, Fine was associated with several dance studios, was a member of the Young Composers' Group, a participant at Yaddo, and a student of Sessions. Fine stated several times: "I had a fixed need to be involved," [19] and from 1964 onward her compositional life escalated. For Fine, her years at Bennington were "marvelous." [20]

Part of the excitement was the opportunity to compose for colleagues. In 1964 she wrote *Song of Persephone for Solo Viola,* which was premièred by Jacob Glick, the violist at Bennington. Musically, *Song of Persephone* is more interesting and dramatic than *Melos.* In turning to Greek legend as inspiration for her music, Fine was still under the influence of Martha Graham, and this was the first time that Fine chose a distinctly feminine theme—the tragedy of the young maiden Persephone and her mother, Demeter. Fine describes the legend on the cover of her piece.

> The legend describes the grief of Kore ("the Maiden," Persephone's name as a young girl) at her abduction by Hades, King of Tartarus. It describes too the grief of her mother, Demeter, who sought Kore for 9 days and nights, calling fruitlessly all the while. As bride of Hades Persephone is the goddess of destruction who sends specters, rules the ghosts and carries into effect the curses of men. In the Spring Persephone is freed from the bowels of the earth and restored to Demeter. The 3 sections of the piece reflect the triadic character of the legend.

Personally, Fine was experiencing a loss because both daughters, who by this time were young women, had left home, and although she did not think of her compositions as ways of relieving her own emotion stress, she did state that her writing was "a kind of diary." [21] Later Fine would write about overtly feminine concerns, such as her operas *Women in the Garden* and the *Memoirs of Uliana Rooney.* Meanwhile she used the challenge of the musical means of a solo viola to express this tragedy. The piece is through-composed. The first section, "Adagio, with intense expressiveness (ca quarter-note = 48)," is Persephone's anguished song. Long descending lines and sudden ascending leaps emphasized by grace notes or sweeping arpeggiated figures reflect the intensity of her horror (see measures 1–4 and 27–31 of ex. 4.5).

Demeter's rage is portrayed by an "Allegro, with bombastic, flambouyant exaggeration and rhythmic elasticity (ca quarter-note = 100)." Although she uses some of her daughter's musical gestures, such as the as-

Example 4.5. Anguish as depicted in first section of the *Song of Persephone* (1964), measures 1–4 and 27–31.

cending grace-note leaps, Demeter's song is a perpetuum mobile reflecting her frustrated and futile search (see ex. 4.6).

The tensions are released in the last short "tranquillo" section, which portrays springtime, when Persephone returns to Demeter. The long graceful legato lines (see ex. 4.7) are a contrast to the previous agitation. Although Fine chose a Greek myth as the inspiration for her piece, its subject matter is contemporary. Reports about abducted and raped daughters are frequent items in the press and media, and Fine's music portrays the emotional horror of these tragedies.

Compositional opportunities escalated now that Fine was a faculty member at Bennington. She composed *Concertino for Piano and Per-*

Example 4.6. Demeter's rage in the second section of the *Song of Persephone* (1964).

Example 4.7. Beginning measures of the third section of the *Song of Persephone* (1964).

Example 4.8. Opening measures of *Concertino for Piano and Percussion Ensemble* (1965) showing shared material.

cussion Ensemble for Paul Price, finishing it in January 1965 and premièring it on March 18, 1965. Fine was the pianist, and Price was well known for his percussion ensemble. She selected mallet instruments (vibraphone, xylophone, and marimba) for her concertino ensemble, adding four timpani and three tam-tams at times for resonant and dramatic effects. Although the *Concertino* is one movement, it is divided into five sections reflecting the usual interpretation of a concertino as a small-scaled concerto: "Allegretto agitato," "Lento appassionato," "Tempi di giga," "Andante tranquillo," and "Moderato." However, Fine blurs the distinction between soloist and ensemble. At times the mallet percussion instruments are an extension of the piano and vice versa. Often the piano and percussion are treated as equals, sharing phrases (see ex. 4.8).

The piano does have a cadenza at the end of the first section, and the "Lento appassionato" features the percussion ensemble, especially the timpani, portraying a seductive dance rhythm, with the piano participating at the end of the section. The *Concertino* is significant because Fine employed two new compositional techniques: she used quotations from her *Alcestis* and inverted retrograde figures. The material from *Alcestis* is hidden—it is first heard at rehearsal letter A, which is an adaptation of measures 8–14 of *Alcestis*'s second movement. The piano in *Concertino*'s last movement, "Moderato" (five measures after rehearsal letter P), presents a more striking quote of *Alcestis*'s beginning theme of rising fourths and repeats the theme again at the ending recapitulative section of this movement (see ex. 4.9). In both instances the quotations are literal; there are no transpositions or other manipulations except the reorchestration. It was at this time that Fine began to consider her compositions as memoirs, and, later, in the *Memoirs of Uliana Rooney,* she would quote liberally from

Example 4.9. Quoted material from *Alcestis* in the "Moderato" section of *Concertino for Piano and Percussion Ensemble* (1965).

her oeuvres. Retrogrades and inversions will be prominent in her later music, also, and Fine experimented with this ordering in the *Concertino*. An inverted figure appears in a two-measure ostinato that accompanies a lyric line. The bottom line is almost an exact inversion of the top, with the exception of the half-step motion from B♭-A not being the whole-step of the G-A above it. The second measure is exact (see ex. 4.10).

This type of ordering is even more apparent in the "Tempi di giga." Inverted retrograde figures are introduced by the piano and appear later in the mallet percussion parts. But it is the last section, "Moderato," in which this ordering is most prominent. Unison rhythms emphasize the pitch patterning so that the percussionists' physical motions while playing the vibraphone and marimba are an analog of the pitch order (see ex. 4.11).

Requests for compositions escalated. José Limón asked that Fine write the music for his dance, *My Song, My Enemy,* which premièred on August 14, 1965, at the Connecticut College American Dance Festival in

Example 4.10. Inverted figures in the ostinato of the first section of *Concertino for Piano and Percussion Ensemble* (1965).

Example 4.11. Inverted retrograde ordering in "Moderato" of *Concertino for Piano and Percussion Ensemble* (1965).

New London, Connecticut. The same year began a period of lecture-recitalist presentations. Fine was a guest at Notre Dame University, the University of Wisconsin at Oshkosh, Bard College in New York, and the College of William and Mary in Richmond, Virginia. Being a faculty member at Bennington validated Fine as a recognized composer.

Requests came from the faculty, too. George Finckel, cellist at Bennington, asked that Fine write a piece for him. At the time she was working on a cantata for voice and orchestra based upon writings by Alcuin (735–804), W. H. Auden (1907–1973), and Pierre Abelard (1079–1142), an eclectic assortment of texts that portray a spiritual questioning about mercy, justice, truth, and the pursuit of peace. Since Finckel was such an expressive cellist, Fine abandoned the cantata format and reshaped her ideas as the *Chamber Concerto for Cello and Six Instruments* (1966), choosing oboe, violin, viola, cello, double bass, and piano to accompany the soloist. However, the idea of the cantata permeates the concerto, which begins with a cello recitative that is followed by three movements, (1) "A Sequence for St. Michael," (2) "Prayer," and (3) "Lament." Short passages of text are inscribed at the beginning of each movement, perhaps as an inspiration to the performers, but what the listener hears is a song without words (see ex. 4.12).

"A Sequence for St. Michael" comprises eight long phrases for the cello with the ensemble occasionally punctuating with fused chords, doubling, a countermelody, or terraced textures that add drama to the cello melody. The short "Declamation," which follows, is for oboe, violin, viola, and double bass. Fine used an articulated oboe melody accompanied by pizzicato string counterpoint to close the supplication to Michael. The passage is marked "with bite," which is followed by an intense "Prayer" inscribed with Auden's text: "O God, put away justice and truth, for we cannot understand them and do not want them. Eternity would bore us dreadfully." [22] The prayer is through-composed featuring passages for solo cello. The *Chamber Concerto* ends with a disturbed "Lament" inspired by the biblical text of David's grieving for his friend Jonathan. The oboe and cello participate as alternating soloists expressing their sorrow.

Being a faculty member at Bennington required some unusual collegial collaborations. One was a project to set various Vermont epithets for chorus. Fine's contribution was "My Sledge and Hammer Ly Reclined" for chorus and instruments. [23] She chose a SATB chorus and an ensemble of six trumpets, six tenor trombones, percussion including two timpani, two pianos, and violin I and II, viola, cello, and double bass to set the following text: "My sledge and hammer ly reclined/My bellows too have lost their wind./My fire's extinct, my forge decayed,/And in the dust my Vise is laid,/My iron's spent, my coals are gone,/My nails are drove, my work is done." The score is humorous, with vocal sounds of "sh—, whinny, clucking, hiss, and whisper" combined with anvil and woodblocks. The brass, pianos, and strings punc-

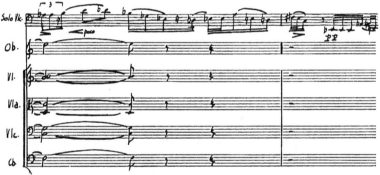

Example 4.12. Beginning measures of *Chamber Concerto for Cello and Six Instruments* (1966) showing melodic writing.

tuate and illustrate the text at appropriate moments. "My Sledge and Hammer Ly Reclined" was premièred on May 26, 1967, at Bennington, and in itself is not a significant work in Fine's catalog; however, she would experiment further with similar vocal and brass sounds in her more successful work, *Paean*.

That same year Fine had an unusual request—the Wykeham Rise School, a private school in Connecticut, wanted a composition for its graduation ceremony. The music was to be in lieu of a commencement speaker. There were no restrictions on Fine's creativity since professional musicians from the Hartt School of Music would be hired for the performance. Fine decided to write *Quintet for Trumpet, String Trio and Harp* (1967). Its five baroque-style movements of "Lento," "Passacaglia," "Duos," "Pavane," and "Cadenza and Ritornella Caleidoscopico" are reminiscent of her piano compositions of the late 1930s, when Fine was studying with Sessions; however, now her sophisticated musical language allowed flexibility. The *Quintet* is experimental while maintaining Fine's personal voice.

The opening "Lento" presents ideas that are used later in the *Quintet*. First, intervals of diminished and stretched octaves (heard as major sevenths and ninths) and diminished and perfect fifths are prominent, allowing the listener an opportunity to reflect upon the material (see ex. 4.13). Then, as a counterpoint evolves amongst the string trio, polyrhythms of 5:4:3 establish a layering of different tempi, which becomes a salient feature of the *Quintet*. Next, a twelve-measure passacaglia theme begins with the viola but soon becomes a *klangfarben* statement amongst the strings (see ex. 4.14). The theme is repeated two more times, and Fine is careful to make its head of a major seventh stand out in the midst of a dense contrapuntal texture. The passacaglia theme has a series of changing meters (7/16, 11/16, 6/16, 7/16, 6/16, 8/16, 10/16 6/16, 7/16, and 6/16) that produces a sinuous and twisting movement that helps to identify its repetition. One only wishes that the "Passacaglia" were longer. Fine's evolving counterpoint, intricate layering, and complex rhythms make this such an interesting movement that the listener is left wanting more.

Two "Duos" follow. The first is between violin and viola. Lacking barlines and meters, this passage exploits the layered tempi heard in the *Quintet*'s beginning. The violin's tempo is sixteenth-note = 184 and marked

Example 4.13. Beginning measures of *Quintet for Trumpet, String Trio and Harp* (1967) showing intervallic choices.

Example 4.14. Beginning measures of "Passacaglia" from *Quintet for Trumpet, String Trio and Harp* (1967).

"with a 'parlando' quality thruout" while the viola's tempo is sixteenth-note = 132 and a "poco espressivo" indication. The lines are independent of each other, and Fine was careful to balance a flourish of activity in one line with longer durations in the other so that the two tempi are more apparent. Together they form a not quite perfect 3/2 ratio (92/66). Further complications in the violin line, such as asymmetrical subdivisions of the beat, make this a virtuostic and challenging movement (see ex. 4.15). The viola continues in the second duet but now its partner is the harp. This duet is less complicated, having meters (although they change frequently), barlines, and common tempo.

The "Pavane" is a somber movement, "Lento, in modo funerale quarter-note = 60," with the trumpet performing a solo four-measure phrase. Thereafter material from the *Quintet*'s "Lento" is reused in differing combinations and rhythms. For example, what was an active cello melody in eighth-, sixteenth-, and thirty-second-notes becomes a slower

Example 4.15. Beginning measures of "Duos" from *Quintet for Trumpet, String Trio and Harp* (1967) showing independent tempi and lines.

trumpet melody augmented in values and at times with extended durations. It is combined with the original viola counterpoint but minus its asymmetrical groupings and changes in dynamics, which make it a more expressive melody than the original. Mutes for both the trumpet and viola also change the character of the melodies. A similar adaptation occurs for a cello passage in measure 151. It was first heard in measure 22. Additional recyclings take place during the "Pavane."

The last movement, "Cadenza and Ritornella Caleidoscopico," begins with a parlando solo for trumpet. Changes in tempi, mutes, and dynamics give it the bravura characteristic that a brass player enjoys. The "Cadenza" is elided to what sounds like a repeat of the *Quintet*'s beginning, and someone familiar with Fine's music would expect a forthcoming closure since a brief recapitulation of initial material has always been part of her formal style. However, Fine has great fun with the "Caleidoscopico" because she recombines materials from previous movements. In measure 201 the violin and viola lines from the "Duos" are switched and layered on top of harp material from the "Pavane." Then in measure 227 a trumpet phrase from the "Passacaglia" is combined with a cello counterpoint that turns out to be a viola passage from the "Lento" beginning. Many more such recombinings occur, and the *Quintet* finally ends with an accompanied version of the trumpet's solo that began the "Pavane." The *Quintet* is so cleverly made that one hopes it spoke to the graduates for whom it was written. Perhaps Fine's selection of movement styles, such as the passacaglia, duos, and pavane, and "Caleidoscopico" ending was her statement to them about life's unexpected twistings and turnings.

Although Fine has no new compositions listed in her catalog for the year 1968, she was busy with a composer-in-residency at the Panorama of the Arts held at the University of Wisconsin, Oshkosh. Later, in the summer, her colleague Jacob Glick premièred the *Song of Persephone for Solo Viola* on August 5 at Lenox, Massachusetts.

Another faculty collaboration occurred in 1969. The Eastman Brass Ensemble suggested to the Bennington composers that they write for their Ensemble. It was a cooperative situation, and a concert was scheduled for April 1, 1970, when the ensemble would perform at Bennington College. Later, selected compositions, including Fine's, would be recorded as "Music From Bennington" on a Composers' Recording Incorporated label (CRI SD 260). Always eager to have an opportunity to write music, Fine decided to compose *Paean* (1969) for narrator-singer (baritone or tenor), women's chorus, and the brass ensemble. She selected isolated texts from "Ode to Apollo" by Keats. Marilyn Bachelder in her study of Fine's music explains the significance of the text: "Keats' *Ode* is itself a paean, a group of songs of rejoicing in honor of Apollo. In the poem, each of nine past poets offers a song for the entertainment of the god. Each of the divergent songs is unsurpassed, but none is universal. But when Apollo joins the combined players, it is his song that proves to be the most beautiful and universal of all." [24]

Fine selected parts of the "Ode" that present trumpet and/or harp imagery associated with the poets Homer, Spenser, and Tasso. Homer's harp and trumpets call to war; Spenser's silver trumpet evokes "a hymn in praise of spotless chastity"; and Tasso's harp beckons "youth from idle slumber, Rousing them from pleasure's lair." *Paean* represents an expansion in Fine's compositional thinking. Although still inspired by Graham's use of Greek mythology (recall Fine's *Alcestis* and *Persephone*), Fine used *Paean* as an opportunity to experiment with aspects of indeterminacy, improvisation (see ex. 4.16), phonetic text, and quarter-tones. In addition, she had not written for a brass ensemble before and chose six trumpets and six trombones. *Paean* begins with a twenty-two-measure passage for brass that resembles keyboard writing. Chords of stacked fourths and registral articulations of seconds set the mood for the forthcoming text. Fine took advantage of dynamic envelopes, usually progressing from soft to loud, and

Example 4.16. Improvisation used in *Paean* (1969).

several mute changes to create color and excitement. The unaccompanied chorus enters using phonemes, such as "ah mm ah uh," and, for the most part, *Paean* moves from incoherent vocal sounds to finally sung text at the end. Spoken passages by the narrator from Keats's text supply the war imagery for the next section of the piece. The chorus interprets these with shaking rising and falling sounds, screams, kissing, whispers, and an improvisation such that "the effect should be one of mass wailing and lamentation" [25] while the brass pursue a martial chordal texture with an occasional melodic passage from the first trumpet. In addition to the beginning, the brass ensemble has several sections alone. One sounds improvised but Fine notated with complex rhythms of 7, 8, and 10 in a 3/4 meter and quasi-serial techniques in which some of the pitches are either permutations, retrograde, or truncated versions of a twelve-note row stated at the beginning of the passage (see ex. 4.17).

Example 4.17. Twelve-tone techniques in *Paean* (1969).

Another is a "fugato ostinato," which is more of an ostinato than a fugato. It begins with a four-measure two-voice counterpoint that becomes an ostinato. Other ostinati of different lengths enter as if they are fugue subjects but continue their repetition. Finally the texture becomes a ten-voice ostinato of varying lengths, somewhat like the "Caleidoscopico" of her *Quintet*. There are two times when Fine reuses the chorus melodies in a trumpet line, probably to establish a cohesiveness, and *Paean* ends recalling its beginning, a favorite closure for Fine.

Fine's music was drawing attention, such that in 1970 Virgil Thomson wrote: "Miss Fine's music, combining emotional intensity with an intellectualized technique, has from the beginning been atonally oriented, though never serial. No rule-of-thumb, no simplified 'method,' no easy short-cut to popularity or fame mars the authenticity of its fine hand work." [26]

NOTES

1. Some of these sketches are published in *The Notebooks of Martha Graham* with an introduction by Nancy Wilson Ross (New York: Harcourt Brace Jovanovich, 1973). For a photograph of the choreography in *Alcestis,* see 214–15 and 359.

2. Robert Sabin reviewed the performance in "Reviews of the Month: Martha Graham and Company," *The Dance Observer,* June–July 1960, 85–86. Sabin's review is an example of uninformed criticism. He wrote: "Vivian Fine's score was something of a disappointment. It is dignified and unobtrusive, but it does not follow the change from winter to spring but retains a wintry pallor throughout." John Martin reviewed the première and wrote, "And the music of Vivian Fine gives it [*Alcestis*] consistent voice. Hearing and seeing emotion and motor response become a unified process" (*New York Times,* April 30, 1960).

3. In 1967 Trampler would première Berio's *Sequenza VI* for viola.

4. Fine was never interested in giving a publisher exclusive rights to her music. Instead, her sister Adelaide reproduced copies of Fine's music when needed using the logo, Catamount Press.

5. The *Fantasy* is not published, but a copy of the manuscript was sent to me by the composer.

6. The *Fantasy* was reviewed as a "strongly structured work . . . of power and originality" by Marion Morrey Richter, "1970 NFMC Parade Concert in New York," *Music Clubs Magazine* 49, no. 4 (Spring 1970): 14, and is quoted by Jones, "Solo Piano Music," on 173.

7. Bertram Turetzky, *The Contemporary Contrabass* (Berkeley: University of California Press, 1974). Although Turetzky uses examples from many composers in his book, Fine's *Melos* is not mentioned.

8. Boepple had founded the Dalcroze School where Sessions taught for a short

while. So, presumably, Boepple knew Fine from her short term as a student there and by reputation through Sessions.

9. Fine made this comment during an interview for a radio program produced for the International League of Women Composers conducted by Ev Grimes.

10. Author's telephone interview with Fine, June 19, 1996. Few women held faculty positions in the 1960s, among them Louise Talma was at Hunter College, and Pauline Oliveros was hired at the University of California, San Diego, in 1968.

11. Fine's situation reflects that of many women faculty at that time. Her position was half-time, and she was already middle-aged. She was a "no risk" hire.

12. Interview, Grimes radio program.

13. Fine, interview with Frances Harmeyer, 1975, 18 quoted by Jones, "Solo Piano Music," 174.

14. For a scientific study of the attitudes, personal characteristics, and political profile of Bennington College, see Theodore Newcomb, Kathryn E. Koenig, Richard Flacks, and Donald Warwick, *Persistence and Change: Bennington College and Its Students after Twenty-five Years* (New York: John Wiley and Son). Unfortunately, the study does not mention the music or arts program.

15. Interview, Grimes radio program.

16. Interview, Grimes radio program.

17. Elizabeth Swados, *Listening Out Loud: Becoming a Composer* (New York: Harper and Row, 1988).

18. Author's telephone interview with Fine, April 8, 1994.

19. Author's telephone interview with Fine, March 9, 1996.

20. Author's telephone interview with Fine, June 19, 1996.

21. Author's telephone interview with Fine, June 19, 1996.

22. This text appears at the bottom of page 12 of the score.

23. Jones, "Solo Piano Music," 174, in footnote 20, points out that Kurt Stone's article about Fine in the *New Grove Dictionary of American Music* lists *My Sledge and Hammer Ly Reclined* as *Epitaph,* which is an incorrect title.

24. Marilyn Meyers Bachelder, "Women in Music Composition: Ruth Crawford Seeger, Peggy Glanville-Hicks, Vivian Fine" (M.A. thesis, Eastern Michigan University, 1973), 119, quoted on 175 of Jones, "Solo Piano Muscle".

25. These directions are given on page 9 of the score.

26. Virgil Thomson, *American Music Since 1910* (New York: Holt, Rinehart, and Winston, 1970), 142–43. This is an especially significant remark from Thomson, whose writings have been criticized as ignoring the accomplishments of women. Note that Thomson was not aware of the serial techniques Fine had used in *The Great Wall of China* and *Paean.*

Chapter 5

Expansion

Part of the "authenticity of its [Fine's compositions'] fine hand work" began to appear in a series of pieces in which Fine expanded her ideas about timbre and texture. Having long ago established her melodic and harmonic atonal vocabulary, she experimented with new freedoms, such as the indeterminacy and improvisation of *Paean*.

Sounds of the Nightingale for soprano, female choral ensemble, and chamber orchestra (1971) is a further step in her expansion of timbre and texture. The piece consists of independent layers of birdsong as portrayed by an ensemble of flute, alto flute, oboe doubling on English horn, clarinet, bass clarinet, French horn, piano, percussion (tuned tom-toms, woodblocks, suspended cymbal, and tissue paper), two violins, two violas, soprano, and the female chorus. Each birdsong is scored meticulously, with appropriate attacks, dynamic changes, and other nuances, to recreate the sounds she wanted. Differing simultaneous tempi, such as quarter-note = 66 for the soprano, 54 for the choral group and piano, 80 for the English horn and strings, and 60 for the French horn (as seen in ex. 5.1), create the layering and independence of materials she desired. Strategic entrances are cued by the conductor, and, at times, entrances are numbered in thick textures to ensure the kinds of timbre and tenure mixtures she wanted. Although the birdsongs are not labeled, Fine's meticulousness resembles that of Messiaen's in scoring birdsong. Nothing is left to chance, and Fine knew exactly what she wanted to hear in her piece.

Soon Fine knew exactly what she needed to further attention to her music. Thomson had written that she was not searching for an "easy shortcut to popularity or fame," but she did notice the burgeoning musical opportunities. It was good fortune for both Bennington and Fine that Jan DeGaetani was on the faculty for a year as a sabbatical replacement, and it was not long before Fine began to compose several pieces for this talented singer. As was Fine's custom, she read widely and found herself attracted to the work of Chilean poet Pablo Neruda (1904–73). She chose two poems, "La Tortuga" and "Oda al Piano." As Fine recalled, the text

Example 5.1. Birdsong textures in *Sounds of the Nightingale* (1971).

"vibrated part of my mind [but] I did not have in mind yet what to do with it."[1] However, soon it became apparent that Jan DeGaetani's voice was the perfect medium for Neruda's text. When asked if George Crumb's "Ancient Voices of Children," which he wrote in 1970 for DeGaetani using Federico García Lorca's poetry, had any influence on Fine's piece, her answer was "no relationship," but she did say that "the timbral sounds were in my head."[2] Associated with these sounds was an underlying sense of humor that becomes apparent near the end of the *Two Neruda Poems*. Fine heard "La Tortuga" as a syllabic chant taking advantage of the dark color of DeGaetani's lower register. At times she is directed to sing "breathy and flat, the voice of an old person" and then return to "nor-

mal voice." Fine used a sparse piano accompaniment that provided guitarlike sounds of plucking, damping, sweeping the strings with fingers,
and slapping the piano case to color the vocal line. The song is through-
composed with an occasional use of a motive C-D^b-G. Example 5.2 illustrates the prescribed change in the singer's voice and some of the guitarlike sounds. The "+" above the tremoloed pitches indicates "press
strings with right hand, play keys with left," and the upward arrow at the
end of the system requires that the "fingers sweep upperhalf [of] low
strings."[3]

Appropriately, "Oda al Piano" is virtuostic for both singer and pianist.
Some of the bravura is prompted by humor—the singer glares angrily at
the pianist and later closes the piano lid, music stand, and finally the
cover, silencing the pianist, who plays the last chord on the closed lid. The
Two Neruda Poems was premièred at Bennington on December 1, 1971,
with Fine accompanying DeGaetani.

During the following year, 1972, Fine made a decision to actively seek
an opportunity she needed—an all-Fine program in New York City. In
recalling this occasion she stated: "I have no talent for building my career. No, I didn't know how to do this. . . . I [would be] sixty-years-old,
and I decided I would take my career in my own hand, and it worked won-
derfully."[4] Actually the *Two Neruda Poems* was a springboard for two
experimental compositions, *Concerto for Piano Strings and Percussion*
(1972) and *Missa Brevis* (1972), which Fine would feature on her forthcoming concert.

It had been twenty years since Fine had written a substantial work for
piano, the *Sinfonia and Fugato* (1952),[5] and having experimented with
some interior piano sounds, such as strumming and plucking in *Two
Neruda Poems,* Fine decided to compose a virtuostic work for herself, the
Concerto for Piano Strings and Percussion (One Performer). The piece
requires an intricate setup using an extra piano stool, timpani, triangle,

Example 5.2. Syllabic chant and guitarlike sounds in "La Tortuga" from *Two
Neruda Poems* (1971).

and cymbal, with appropriate notation for plucking, stopping, scratching, bouncing, and performing clusters on the strings. Recall that in her teen years during the 1920s Fine performed some of Cowell's compositions, such as the *Aeoline Harp* and *Banshee,* so one wonders why she waited so long to write her own experimental keyboard piece. When asked, her reply was, "I don't know . . . [and] the idiom [Cowell's pieces] did not influence [me] but his boldness [did] . . . people were aghast and laughed."[6]

The *Concerto* exploits pianistic technique to the fullest by transferring piano gestures to various parts of the instruments. The *Concerto* begins with resounding bounced, plucked, and scratched interior sounds that gradually move to pentatonic keyboard rifts in contrary motion (see ex. 5.3). Gradually the performer's movements incorporate the percussion instruments that surround the piano. Fine reported that it is not long before the audience is befuddled and begins to wonder who is the

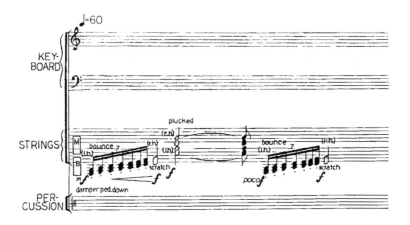

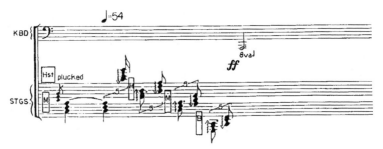

Example 5.3. Interior string and keyboard sounds in *Concerto for Piano Strings and Percussion (One Performer),* (1972).

soloist in this *Concerto*—the keyboard, strings, or percussion?[7] By page 6 of the manuscript, several minutes into the piece, Fine quotes Bach's first two-part invention. It begins with the opening motive played on the keyboard and then transfers to the interior with the following instructions: "Play firmly on strings with fingers. Exact pitches are not required, but play in the indicated register and keep the relative relationships indicated."[8] It is at this point that the audience realizes that the piece is a spoof and begins to appreciate Fine's humor. Since she wrote it for herself, she incorporated all of her own virtuostic technique, which she executed seriously, so that her performance became a theater piece. In fact, it was so difficult to play, Fine memorized it.[9] The piece is well made with exact performance details, and frequent tempo changes (twenty-seven) shape the material. There is no improvisatory or aleatoric procedure. Instead, gestures are expanded, and an impressive keyboard cadenza precedes a short recapitulation.

In preparing for her concert, Fine envisioned another composition, something for cellos and voice.[10] The inspiration came when she heard Finckel's cello students play transcriptions of Bach's Chorales. Finckel probably used this repertoire to build intonation and ensemble playing. Fine liked the sound and thought she would incorporate it with the improvisation skills that Baker was using with his vocal students. Originally the piece was to be *Transformations;* however, she changed her mind and rewrote the vocal parts for Jan DeGaetani, and decided that it was time to explore the medium of prerecorded tape. Her piece became *Missa Brevis for Four Cellos and Taped Voice* (1972). Instead of using improvisation, Fine composed four vocal parts and, with the help of Joel Chadabi, recorded DeGaetani singing each part. Then Fine decided how these separate tracks were to be combined and used in conjunction with the cellos.[11] Fine's *Missa* is a hybrid of ten sections: (1) "Praeludium," (2) "Kyrie," (3) "Omnium," (4) "Visibilium omnium et invisibilium," (5) "Lacrymosa," (6) "Teste David cum Sibylla," (7) "Dies Irae," (8) "Eli, Eli, lomo asov toni," (9) "Sanctus," and (10) "Omein," and, obviously, is not liturgical. There are no quotations, such as the *Dies Irae* motif of which composers have been so fond. This was the first time Fine chose a sacred text for her music. Others would follow. Composing the *Missa* was her way of exploring Christian spirituality, and she selected a variety of texts, true to her acknowledgment, "I am a taker."[12]

The *Missa* is recorded on CRI SD 434, and the listener experiences it as a sophisticated and musical use of the voice. One would not know the voice is entirely prerecorded, and that the cellos are live. Just the opposite would be expected. Frequently the cellos function as a pipe organ, providing a thick chordal or cluster texture that is heard alone, as in the slowly changing and beating chords of "Praeludium." The "Kyrie," which follows, is an a capella three-part vocal counterpoint of DeGae-

tani's voice, never in imitation, but contrasting and elegant lines that are
the hallmark of Fine's music. The text is a repetition of one word, *Kyrie,*
not the traditional liturgical setting. "Omnium" has an aleatoric aspect in
that the cellists, after having a cued entrance, are free "to keep their own
time"[13] but are given specific material featuring rapidly changing dynamic envelopes resulting in a cluster texture. Again, just a single word,
omnium, is presented on the tape, and the superimposition of the voice
parts resembles the slowly changing chords heard in "Praeludium." The
closing cello section of "Omnium" is a dense and dissonant texture of
muted double stops and trills that forecast later moments in *Missa Brevis.* Some of this tension is relieved with a presto four-voice polytonal
canon for the cellos, with the leading voice in C major and other entrances
in D♭, D, and E♭. The resulting commotion portrays "Visibilium omnium
et invisibilium" of this textless section.

The tape again remains silent for "Lacrymosa" when the cellos assume
vocal characteristics for a motetlike texture for the cello "Lacrymosa"
(see ex. 5.4). Cellos two and one are in canon; cello three is a retrograde
of cello two; and cello four's gestures are a reversal of the original canon
and present an upward sighing motion that increases in dynamics. It is

Example 5.4. Imitative counterpoint in "Lacrymosa" in *Missa Brevis* (1972).

followed by eerie chordal cello harmonics, which create the atmosphere for "Teste David cum Sibylla," to which DeGaetani's voice adds vocal tremors and nonpitched whispers. Fine presents the "Dies Irae" as dramatic, harsh energy, which was alluded to earlier. The cellos begin with a chaconne of dissonant, down-bowed, grim chords. The voice enters at the second repetition of the chaconne,[14] which is slower, slightly disjointed, and elongated by measures of rest. Glissandi and an even slower tempo mark the third repetition, while the original tempo with a rhythmic change to a 6/8 meter announces the final statement. The drama intensifies when DeGaetani's voice is first heard alone in a Hebrewlike chant for "Eli, Eli, lomo asov toni" (My God, why has thou forsaken me), which through tape manipulation becomes a dense vocal texture. "Sanctus" relieves the tension as the cellos perform lyrical lines somewhat reminiscent of the previous chantlike "Eli, Eli." "Omein" features a more traditional voice with chordal accompaniment, and *Missa Brevis* closes with a dissonant chord that suggests that although the music ends, thoughts about it continue. Part of the success of *Missa Brevis* is Fine's good judgment about elision and proportion. Often sustained cello chords link sections, coordinating and masking the beginnings and endings of taped material. Never does a section seem too long, and frequently the listener would like to hear more.[15]

Fine returned to birdsong for an unusual piece, *The Flicker* for solo flute or piano right hand (1973).[16] Her flicker (a woodpecker) sings virtuosic lines that change continuously for this long six-page solo (see ex. 5.5). One would expect some type of reuse of material to account for the multiplicity of pitches, but this is not the case. Fine reported that she "wrote what I heard,"[17] which was the imagined flight and song of this active bird. Again she added a touch of humor with the following direction, which ends the piece: "Performer slowly lifts and turns head and

Example 5.5. Virtuosic lines in *The Flicker* (1973). (Copyright © 1981 by Gun-Mar Music, Inc.; used with permission.)

eyes as if following an ascending trajectory disappearing into space, hold final position for a moment."[18]

Fine's career expanded several ways during 1973. Composers Recording Incorporated had released the first professional recording of one of her compositions, *Concertante for Piano and Orchestra,* performed by the Japan Philharmonic Symphony Orchestra, conducted by Akeo Watanabe, with Reiko Honsho as pianist. Then, on March 11, the radio station WNYC broadcasted this recording plus taped performances of *Paean* and *Alcestis.* The next month, April, included an even more important event—the first all-Fine concert. She rented the Finch Auditorium, which is part of a women's college in New York City, for one hundred dollars[19] and designed her program to include *Missa Brevis,* the *Concerto for Piano Strings and Percussion (One Performer), Two Neruda Poems,* and the *Confession.* It was a turning point, which Fine described this way:

> Things changed around in 1973 when I arranged a concert of my music in New York. That's what turned things around. It was reviewed in The [*New York*] *Times* by Donal Henahan. It was a laudatory review. From then on my career blossomed. At that time I decided I was not going to depend on other people to play my music. I would arrange it. . . . I was sixty-years-old, and I decided I would take my career in my own hands, and it worked wonderfully.[20]

Henahan's review began with the caveat:

> A complete program of anybody's music can be too much, even if the anybody is a Bach, or a Beethoven who has been unlucky enough to attract a mediocre performer's undivided attention. But a concert of Vivian Fine's compositions at Finch College Concert Hall on Sunday night proved all too short, for two good reasons: She writes elegant and inventive works, and Jan DeGaetani thinks highly enough of them to pour her remarkable talent unstintingly into them.[21]

More opportunities emerged in 1974. Fine mentioned to one of the New York Public Library's staff that she had some interesting dance memorabilia. Soon the library honored her with an exhibit, "Vivian Fine and Five Dancers," which was a display of dance composition manuscripts she had done in the past. Then she applied for and received a National Endowment for the Arts (NEA) Grant. She was taking charge.

The grant resulted in *Teisho* for eight singers or small chorus and string quartet (1975). Bennington College was opening a new Arts Center, and Fine wanted an opportunity to present a composition for this occasion. It would be premièred by the Sine Nomine Singers and the Bennington College Contemporary Quartet conducted by Fine. Since the singers were professionals and Fine would be conducting (see fig. 5.1), she wrote a difficult and complicated piece of 124 manuscript pages. Although no electronics are involved, *Teisho*'s layerings, texture manipulation, and advanced string writing resemble ideas Fine experimented with in *Missa Brevis*. Also, both pieces reflect her spiritual inquiries at the

Figure 5.1. Fine conducting the première of *Teisho*.

time. Zen training was becoming much more available in the United States during the mid-1970s, and Fine, a voracious reader, explored some of D. T. Suzuki's writings and selected several Zen stories to set to music. As indicated on the score, "Teisho are the sermons or talks delivered by the Zen masters to the disciples." Often a teisho involves a puzzle that is difficult for the listener to comprehend, and Fine's *Teisho* is no exception. For her it was an opportunity to be "interested in two kinds of time, seamless and measured."[22]

Teisho begins with a dense, dissonant four-voice canon for the string quartet, a busy texture she had used in previous compositions. However, this material is more sophisticated because it becomes the basis for much of the string writing and some of the vocal lines, providing an economy to this complex work. The canons are first presented as noteheads grouped in phrases with the direction of "M.M.69, six notes per tick" (see ex. 5.6), but gradually rhythmic patterns and polyrhythmic textures of 2, 3, 4, and 5 emerge; large sections are used in retrograde; instruments exchange lines; prolation canons develop; and original pitches become transformed as string harmonics. Similar techniques, such as canons, retrogrades, and even inversions, are used with the voices, making the text (sometimes in a seven- or eight-part setting) difficult to hear and understand, which seems appropriate, since words of wisdom need to be repeated, and though heard, are generally perplexing.

Fine divided her composition into two parts and chose three texts for part one: "The Stringless Harp," "With the Passing of Winter," "Let the Difference Be Even a Tenth of an Inch" and three texts for part two: "If people ask me what Zen is like I will say that it is like learning the art of burglary," "The King of Good Memory," and "The Ten Thousand Things." *Teisho* is continuous, with only a slight pause between parts one and two. Careful elisions join the ending of one text to the beginning of the next. A change in meter and rhythmic texture announces a new text; for example, "Let the Difference Be Even a Tenth of an Inch" begins with a ho-

Example 5.6. Beginning canons in *Teisho* (1975).

mophonic four-part chorus in a 3/4 meter accompanied by string harmonics in 6/8 whose pitches are from the original canon (see ex. 5.7). The string writing is the most experimental, with dense high harmonics sounding like wind chimes and a pizzicato texture doubling the voices in "The King of Good Memory" suggesting a sitar, which seems appropriate to the text "I know there is a mantram in one of the Sutras."

Fine experimented even further with texture and time in *Meeting for Equal Rights 1866, a Cantata for Chorus, Orchestra, Mezzo Soprano, Baritone, and Narrator* (1975). The circumstances surrounding this piece are unusual. Originally personnel from the Cooper Union for the Advancement of Science and Art in New York City asked Fine if she would be a consultant for a commissioned project, a celebration of the historic meeting for equal rights. This meeting addressed the question of whether the Civil Rights Act, which gave voting rights to males, including black men, should also grant women, both black and white, the vote. Since in 1976 the country was celebrating its bicentennial, it was especially appropriate to examine the issue of equal rights. After some consideration, Fine decided that she wanted to do the project because she had an idea—she would compile writings and speeches from the period of the original meeting for equal rights and set these to music in the form of a cantata with soloists and a narrator. She wanted her music to portray the masses that gathered for the meeting, so she designed the cantata in three movements; divided the orchestra into three sections; and assigned each its

Example 5.7. Change in texture for beginning of new text in *Teisho* (1975).

own conductor. The movements would be performed simultaneously. In a 1975 interview with Frances Harmeyer, Fine discussed some of the suffragettes' feelings at the time:

> *Meeting* revolves around the fourteenth amendment and the time of the Civil War. . . . I just came upon this reading casually—a fact which is know[n] to any historian—that after the Civil War there was a split among the Abolitionists. The men wanted to give the black man, the freed black man, the vote, but they refused to give it to the women. The women abolitionists, like Elizabeth Cady Stanton and Susan B. Anthony, all of them were outraged, that [after] their work to free the black man, they were to be denied the vote, both black and white women. This was an intensely passionate struggle, a really great moment and heroic period of the suffrage movement.[23]

Her ambitious project required a research assistant, and money was available since the project would be funded by the National Endowment for the Arts. Fine hired Gail Parker, who located texts with passages by such speakers as Catherine Beecher, Elizabeth Cady Stanton, the National Woman's Rights Central Committee, Robert Purvis, Horace Greeley, Senator Frelinghysen of New Jersey, and Frederick Douglass, among others.[24] After the introduction, the chorus is segregated, with the men first singing in chorale style (see ex. 5.8) and at times becoming a speak-

Example 5.8. Men's chorale from *Meeting for Equal Rights 1866* (1975).

ing chorus accompanied by strings. At one point the men's chorus sings these words of Senator Frelinghuysen:

> It seems as if the God of our race has stamped upon the women of this country a milder, gentler nature. They have a higher and holier mission. Their mission is at home, by their blandishments and their love to assuage the passions of men as they come from the battle of life.[25]

The women have more active and varied textures accompanied by the brass and winds. Example 5.9 is the section of the women's chorus with the text "By contest and discord she shall carry her points," words of Catherine Beecher, which in Fine's *Meeting* turn into gibberish. This passage is juxtaposed with the men's chorale in example 5.9.

Each has a different tempo, which helps to maintain the separation — the men's is quarter-note = 56 while the women's is quarter-note = 88. The soloists and narrator form a third group, which is often punctuated by percussion. They sing or speak for equal rights and women's vote. The narrator ends the cantata with these words by Laura Curtis Bullard:

> It was a glorious day for this republic when she shook herself free from disgrace of negro slavery, and declaring that she would have no subject race within her boundaries, broke the chain of four million bondsmen! It will be a still more glorious day in her annals

Example 5.9. Women's chorus singing text that turns to gibberish in *Meeting for Equal Rights 1866* (1975).

when the republic shall declare the injustice of a slavery of sex, and shall set free her millions of bond women.

It is difficult to determine the composite mix since the score has minimal instructions about how the conductors coordinate the movements, and there is no tape of the performance. However, Fine knew exactly what she wanted. When asked about its première, Fine replied, "Some liked it; some didn't."[26] Byron Belt did and wrote the following review for the *Long Island Press:*

> Vivian Fine's *Meeting for Equal Rights 1866* proved a stirring and timely piece devoted to the unhappily still struggling cause of Equal Rights. Taking a feminist viewpoint that is full of righteous rage—which is understandable—and composition—which is more important—*Meeting for Equal Rights 1866* provides the first current artistic statement for women's rights other than literature.
>
> While various painters, choreographers and others in the performing arts have made spasmodic treatment of women, Vivian Fine has selected the writings and spoken words of both men and women and set them to music that augments and dramatizes the conflicts and hopes of countless generations.
>
> Lyndon Woodside and the Oratorio Society had given an April world première of *Meeting for Equal Rights 1866* in the historic setting of the Cooper Union Great Hall. On that occasion the scoring was for full orchestra. The conductor wished to repeat Miss Fine's important work, and asked the composer to rescore it for organ, percussion and winds, which she did—with tremendous success.
>
> Vivian Fine's cantata is an eclectic score that manages to be obviously descriptive of textual matters. . . . The chaos of discordant words is captured by multiple text being shouted, recited and sung, with instrumental shrieks from the organ and winds aside vivid color.[27]

It was not unusual for Fine to assemble texts and set them to music, but using feminist writings and promoting women was new. Two operas, *Women in the Garden* and the *Memoirs of Uliana Rooney,* would continue this direction.

Fine returned to her earlier and less complex style for *Romantic Ode for String Orchestra with solo violin, viola, and cello* (1976). It was commissioned by the Chamber Music Conference and Composers Forum of the East, and Fine took this opportunity to write her lyric contrapuntal lines, which are so successful for strings. At first the solo trio is accompanied by the string orchestra, but later the two merge and become a massed ensemble, a sound that Fine enjoys: "I like that luscious, full string sound. . . . There's nothing quite as satisfying as having all the strings . . . playing at once."[28]

Fine even returned to some of her earlier music for *Sonnets for Baritone and Orchestra* (1976). The sonnets, "To one who has long in city past," "On the Sea," and "To a Cat," are by Keats. Numbers one and three are sketches from 1939, which she reworked, setting them for a large orchestra. The music is easily accessible since it was commissioned by the Sage City Symphony, and the performers must have enjoyed her colorful orchestration, especially "To a Cat" (see ex. 5.10). Her ease and freedom in writing for a large ensemble are indicative of an experienced composer, one who has evolved from the earlier use of the orchestra as woodwind, brass, and string choirs in *Concertante for Piano and Orchestra* to a fluid mixing and contrasting of instruments as used in the *Sonnets*.

Although the *Romantic Ode* and *Sonnets* were smaller works, Fine's creativity was expanding. She applied for another NEA grant with the idea that she would do a project involving nineteenth-century feminist texts. Obviously *Meeting for Equal Rights* prompted this desire to know more about the women's movement. Fine recalls taking twenty books when she and her husband went on a vacation in Mexico so she could locate texts for her project.[29] Gradually she simplified her plan and selected writings of four women and realized that she had the ingredients for an opera. The characters were: Isadora Duncan (dramatic soprano), Virginia Woolf (lyric soprano), Emily Dickinson (mezzo-soprano), Gertrude Stein (contralto or dark mezzo), and a tenor. The instumentation was practical: flute, B♭ clarinet, bassoon, piano, viola, cello, double bass, and two percussionists playing a varienty of instruments for added color. The setting was simple and appropriate—a garden—and her opera would last about an hour. In an interview with Elizabeth Vercoe, Fine discussed its origins.

> I myself have found since the '60s that the woman's movement has been a liberating influence for me personally—to realize how men treat women, how women react to being treated by men. . . . So it came very naturally and seemed perfectly natural to have an all-women opera with one character called the Tenor. It certainly has to do with women's feelings, the bonding of women and the things they have had to endure. For instance, at one point in *Women in the Garden* there is a quotation from Emily Dickinson of scenes of her own death. She says, "When I died, the clerk recorded it in the town ledger as Emily Dickinson, at home." It means that she was taking care of her father. Not [Emily Dickinson] a poet. And then Isadora Duncan was treated so terribly by Gordon Craig, and that's in there too. He is saying, "My work, my work; why do you have to go on

Example 5.10. Orchestration in *Sonnets for Baritone and Orchestra* (1976).

the stage and wave your arms!" He wrote this to her in a letter. . . . She suffered a great deal from that. . . . Gertrude Stein is the philosopher, as she usually is. The tenor at one point is kind of Picasso; he's her friend. And there is a long episode . . . from Virginia Woolf from *A Room of One's Own*. I hope I did it with a light hand, but all those concerns were real and they *are* real.[30]

Some of the concerns are: career, philosophy, sorrow, pain, relationship to father and mother, depression, Jewishness, money, composing, and romance. Thus, Fine's opera is about thoughts and emotions rather than actions. There are no arias or dances. There are no complicated layerings or combining of different tempi as in the *Meeting for Equal Rights.* Instead, each character sings alone, and then in duets, sometimes in trios, and occasionally a quartet. Fine did not write the libretto out first—she assembled her text as she went along, and when asked what her feelings were about *Women in the Garden,* she replied: "I feel good about it" and then recalled that she had written the music and libretto together and maybe that was why "it went extremely well."[31]

In the beginning each person has a solo in which she introduces herself. Gertrude Stein is first and reminds us, "In the month of February were born Washington, Lincoln and I."[32] Emily Dickinson states, "We must be careful what we say. No bird resumes its nest."[33] Isadora Duncan wants the audience to know "I was born by the sea, and I have noticed that all the great events of my life have taken place by the sea,"[34] and Virginia Woolf reveals her interest immediately: "But one could perhaps go a little deeper into the question of novel writing and the effect of sex upon the novelist."[35] The tenor has multiple roles. At first he writes a letter to Emily as presumably a male friend; then he is her father. When Isadora Duncan is singing, the tenor becomes Gordon Craig, and as Fine mentioned in the interview, he is also Stein's friend, Picasso. However, the tenor never interacts with Virginia Woolf.

Fine chose not to specify staging, costuming,[36] or production concerns about her opera, deciding to let the directors handle those issues. She had learned: "They like to do that."[37] Instead she focused her attention upon composing the libretto, making textural overlays in duets, such as Emily Dickinson's concern that her obituary would list "Occupation: At home"[38] while Gertrude Stein counterpoints that thought with "Man is man was man will be gregarious and solitary."[39] In a trio, which follows (see ex. 5.11), Dickinson is still concerned about her occupation; Stein philosophizes, "He will be [gregarious] because it is his nature to be"; and Woolf prophesies, "The time approaches when these soliloquies shall be shared. We shall not always give out a sound like a beaten gong."[40] Fine is careful to write a thin accompaniment so that the text can be heard. The strings' snapped pizzicato passage and the woodwinds' repeated F's support the voices lightly, and Stein's text, which has been heard previously, uses the same melody.

Not surprisingly, Fine selected this passage from Virginia Woolf's *A Room of One's Own:* "The woman composer stands where the actress stood in the time of Shakespeare. So does history accurately repeat itself."[41] Then Fine combines this passage in an unaccompanied duet between Stein and Woolf (see ex. 5.12).

Example 5.11. Trio among Woolf, Dickinson, and Stein from scene two of *Women in the Garden* (1977).

Women in the Garden has many influences of Fine's earlier work *A Guide to the Life Expectancy of a Rose* in terms of texture and clarity but minus the humor. By 1977 Fine used her composition to explore her sensitivities about women artists and the feminist movement. Stephanie Von Buchau wrote in *Opera News* that *Women in the Garden* is "a remarkable contemporary work, with a tintinnabulating orchestral score of delicate beauty, thoroughly idiomatic (if difficult) vocal lines, emotional

Example 5.12. Duet between Stein and Woolf referring to the role of a woman composer from *Women in the Garden* (1977).

penetration and a civilized, wholesome warmth. . . . A feminist piece by definition . . . does not preach or rage and concentrates on the positive aspects of sisterhood."[42] *Women in the Garden* was premièred February 12, 1978, by the Port Costa Players conducted by Alan Balter at San Francisco, California, and reviewed by Charles Shere in *High Fidelity/Musical America,* June 1978. Shere reported:

> Vivian Fine's opera *The Women in the Garden* drew capacity houses in its three first performances in San Francisco and Oakland in February, and earned standing ovations for its composer. . . . The libretto suggests extended recitative, and *The Women in the Garden* is clearly in the operatic tradition of Wagner and Debussy, not Verdi and Puccini.
>
> In fact, the clearest musical influence on this hour-long stage poem is Erik Satie's *Socrate,* that gentle musical commentary on the death of Socrates. Like Satie, Fine shapes the drama simply, setting forth long extended sections with little internal articulation. The musical effect is cumulative: *The Women in the Garden* does not pull the audience along with a succession of contrasting numbers, but convinces them with patient, logical, graceful musical statement. . . .
>
> The music becomes chordal, expressing the joy of life and the will to live freely. Throughout, rhythmic patterns proceed simply, now falling on a common beat, now going their own ways, following ideas in Messiaen and Ives to express the mutual support of diverse voices.[43]

Later in his review, Shere had harsh comments for some local critics:

> The critics from the two San Francisco papers chose to leave early, noisily by some accounts, and dismissed the work in no uncertain

terms. Reached later, they explained that they knew within five minutes that they weren't going to like the piece, and could see how it
would continue without actually having to remain in attendance.
(They had journeyed together to the opera.) Miss Fine, who teaches
at Bennington, was dismissed as writing academic music from an
"ivory tower." Her work was "not an opera" because it lacked action
and drama. Noting from program notes that she had composed ex-
tensively for the dance, she was referred to as perhaps a ballet composer, certainly not yet ready for opera. One critic suggested that *The
Women* might work as a song cycle, after the piece of Virgil Thomson's *Capital, Capitals*—a piece for four male voices with not a song
in it! And, finally, it was complained that texts could not be understood because of the high tessitura of the (necessarily) female voice.

Such remarks will add fuel to the arguments of those who see
masculine condescension in the attitude of some San Francisco critics. What's worse is the continued assumption by newspaper critics that they needn't bother to look at score, to understand the intentions of the work they deal with, or even to attend all of the event
in question before writing their reviews. It's a disheartening commentary on the state of the cultural life of a major center.[44]

The following year, 1978, Fine's inspiration expanded further, and she
explored another realm of compositional technique—quotation.[45] She
did not use literal quotation but chose gestures, such as shapes from Schubert's *Moments musicaux* as the basis for her *Momenti* (1978) for piano
solo written in honor of the 150th anniversary of Schubert's death and
dedicated to Roger Sessions.[46] Jones studied and wrote about Fine's *Momenti* in detail, comparing her music to Schubert's, and anyone performing the *Momenti* should consult Jones's work.[47] The six short movements, which Fine wrote from April to June, were inspired by Schubert's
gestures and not until the end of the last movement is there an actual
quote. The gestures become transformed into Fine's music, which sounds
un-self-conscious in its free use of dissonance and vigorous in the frequent changes in rhythmic groupings. Of special interest to the future direction of Fine's music is Moment Five, a toccata texture in which Jones
noticed Fine's use of canon and retrograde (see ex. 5.13).

It was not long before Fine had another project, a request from the Metropolitan Brass Quartet of New York City. The piece, *Quartet for Brass*, is
scored for two trumpets, horn, and bass trombone. Each of the *Quartet*'s
four movements explores a specific idea, and the brass ensemble is heard
in differing contexts. For example, in "Variations," the first movement,
Fine creates a stark intervallic texture, which later becomes a retrograde
(see ex. 5.14) and then accumulates energy by doubling its speed. Fine is
careful to emphasize the retrograde with a change in tempo, removal of

Example 5.13. Beginning measures of Moment Five from *Momenti* (1978). (Copyright © 1983 by GunMar Music, Inc.; used with permission.)

Example 5.14. Retrograde in "Variations" from *Quartet for Brass* (1978). (Copyright © 1985 by GunMar Music, Inc.; used with permission.)

mutes, and accented dynamics. The ensemble becomes more brasslike for the second movement, "Fanfare," in which the listener hears various pairings of the instruments in a contrapuntal texture that is meticulously shaped through dynamics, attacks, and, at times, microtonal tuning. "Eclogue" is quiet and sparse with solo instrumental lines. The ending is a prolonged C that is colored by changes in dynamics and mutes. The fourth movement,

"Variations," becomes more lively as the ensemble presents individual and unison lines that punctuate the rapidly changing rhythmic patterns. "Variations" is constantly dancing. Material is reused as canons, retrogrades, and in augmentation, but the energy never ceases, and the listener does not have time to register the compositional manipulations.

The *Quartet*'s contrapuntal devices and *Momenti*'s gestural quotations are even more prominent in *Lieder for Viola and Piano* (1978). Earlier Fine wrote the *Song of Persephone for Solo Viola*, which her colleague, Jacob Glick, premièred August 5, 1968, at Lenox, Massachusetts. Fine offered to write another piece, the *Lieder,* for Glick, and "he was delighted."[48] Noticing that she was drawn more and more to vocal forms, Fine used gestural ideas from some of Hugo Wolf's and Schubert's songs for her *Lieder*. There are six short movements, all written within the period of one month, November 10 to December 4. Each movement's gesture is stated clearly and then manipulated contrapuntally, such as the piano's beginning gesture in example 5.15 later stated in retrograde inversion while the viola's melody is independent of these manipulations. The complexity increases in movement two when the viola repeats its beginning melody, which is juxtaposed with a retrograde of the piano part that is played several octaves higher than the original. In other movements the viola has retrograde fragments or is integrated with the piano's texture because both

Example 5.15. Beginning measures of *Lieder for Viola and Piano* (1978).

Example 5.16. Prolation canon between the viola and piano in Movement Five of *Lieder for Viola and Piano* (1978).

instruments have similar gestures and rolled chords. Movement five features a repetition of the viola's beginning melody later in a three-voice prolation canon between the viola and piano (see ex. 5.16).

Movement six is the most highly integrated. The viola and piano exchange material and participate in retrograde action, and finally an augmented retrograde closes the *Lieder for Viola and Piano*. For Fine the use of these contrapuntal devices, such as canon and retrograde, were not just easy ways to generate more music, but a natural expansion of already well-made melodies. When asked if, after writing a melody, she could she read it backward and mentally hear the retrograde, her answer was "Yes!"[49]

Having completed *Women in the Garden,* Fine was involved in another large project, *For a Bust of Erik Satie: A Short Mass* (1979). Harry Mathews, a professor in the French department at Bennington, wanted to do an interdisciplinary production that would be part of the celebration for a new art building at the college. Mathews translated text by Georges Guy concerning Erik Satie, which Fine set as *Mass* for soprano, contralto (or mezzo), narrator(s), flute, bassoon, trumpet, trombone, cello, and double bass. Her *Mass* is a setting of the Proper with sections titled "Introit," "Psalm," "Collect," "Gradual," "Tract," "Sequence," "Gospel," and "Secret." Three narrators from the drama department, who, according to Fine, were over six feet tall,[50] delivered most of the text, sometimes in English, sometimes in French, and often in translation. The *Mass* begins with the following solo narration: "Since most of what follows is doggerel, and unrhymed doggerel at that, its performance should be kept within the bounds of a not unpleasant monotony, highlighted occasionally with touches of greater melancholy. A note of seriousness imbued with piety would also be appropriate."[51]

Fine's music captures the spirit of the text perfectly. She wrote simple syllabic melodies accompanied by a one- or two-part instrumental counterpoint, and purely ensemble sections often repeat previously heard vocal lines. The "Collect," which is spoken by two narrators, ends with the following: "Deliver not thy servant Erik unto the power of Paris Opera houses, but may all Thy holy angels receive him into the Metropolitan Art church of Jesus, the leader he so longed to find."[52]

Nightingales—Motet for Six Instruments (1979) was Fine's final piece for the year, another commission by the Chamber Music Conference and Composers Forum of the East. She continued the theme of expansion by using a vocal form for an instrumental ensemble of flute, oboe, violin, two violas, and double bass. The score, which has no relationship to her earlier *Sounds of the Nightingale* (1971), is inscribed with the following: "What bird so sings yet so does wail?/ O tis the ravish'd nightingale" by John Lyly, a poet whose work she had used about forty years prior in *Four Elizabethan Songs.* Instead of words, this motet has five nightingalelike melodies, with the flute presenting melody one, the oboe having melody two three beats later, the violin sounding melody three during a repetition of the oboe's melody, the viola beginning melody four at the end of the violin's melody three, and the double bass introducing melody five later. The ensemble is instructed to "Sing like a nightingale,"[53] and each melody is so distinctive that it could represent a line of poetry. Like in *Quartet* and other recent pieces, Fine recycles the lines, recombining (such as having the oboe perform melody five while the double bass has melody four) and using retrograde forms, which are easily recognized due to reversed dotted rhythms and so on.

By this time Fine's talent was so well developed and flexible that she could write a highly textured and complex *Missa Brevis* for four celli and tape and then several years later collaborate interdisciplinary projects and compose minimalistic-like music for *For a Bust of Erik Satie* or substitute birdsong for words in a motet. In each situation her acute hearing and musicality instinctively dictate music that is appropriate. Other musicians recognized her abilities, too, and the number of commissions increased.

NOTES

1. Author's telephone interview with Fine, August 14, 1996.

2. Recall that these questions were asked when Fine was over eighty years old. Although *Two Neruda Poems* bears some resemblance to Crumb's work, the recording for "Ancient Voices of Children" was produced in 1971, the year Fine wrote her pieces. It is quite possible she had not heard Crumb's composition.

3. This information is taken from the score.

4. Author's telephone interview with Fine, June 17, 1994.

5. In 1966 she composed *Four Piano Pieces* for which the manuscript is not available.

6. Author's telephone interview with Fine, August 14, 1996.

7. Author's telephone interview with Fine, November 7, 1996.

8. *Concerto for Piano Strings and Percussion,* page 1 of the score.

9. Author's telephone interview with Fine, November 7, 1996.

10. Author's telephone interview with Fine, December 5, 1995.

11. Author's telephone interview with Fine, February 14, 1997.

12. Author's telephone interview with Fine, December 5, 1995.

13. This instruction is on page 3 of the score.

14. There is an error in the third measure of system three. The B in cello four's line should be a $B^\flat$, as it is in all other repetitions of the chaconne.

15. Robert Commanday reviewed a 1990 performance of the *Missa Brevis* at the Composers Incorporated concert in the Veterans Building Green Room in San Francisco. He found the work "curious, and visionary . . . highly personal . . . [but] left touching moments and a sense of sketchiness and incompletion" (*The San Francisco Chronicle,* October 4, 1990).

16. At first, Fine titled the piece *The Second Prophet Bird* and later changed it to *The Flicker.*

17. Author's telephone interview with Fine, June 12, 1997.

18. This direction appears on page 6 of the score.

19. Author's telephone interview with Fine, May 9, 1997.

20. Author's telephone interview with Fine, June 17, 1994.

21. Donal Henahan, "Concert," *New York Times,* April 12, 1973.

22. Author's telephone interview with Fine, July 1, 1994.

23. Quoted by Jones, "Solo Piano Music," 179. The italics are not acknowledged, but, presumably, they were added by Harmeyer to reflect Fine's intonation.

24. This information is from the libretto that accompanied the piece's première.

25. Neither the score nor the libretto indicates the text's source.

26. Author's telephone interview with Fine, May 29, 1997. Henahan was one critic who did not like it, writing, "The choral writing is drab and lumpy when it is not drab and spiky" ("Concert: Oratorio Society Sings Equal-Rights Cantata," *New York Times,* May 22, 1976).

27. Byron Belt, review in the *Long Island Press,* May 21, 1976, quoted in LePage, 85–86, and Jones, "Solo Piano Music," 180. Donal Henahan also reviewed the concert for the *New York Times,* May 22, 1976, and found the work lacking lyric impulse and drama.

28. Elinor Armer, "A Conversation with Vivian Fine: Two Composers Talk Shop," *Strings,* March/April 1991, 74.

29. Author's telephone interview with Fine, May 29, 1997.

30. Elizabeth Vercoe, "Interview with Composer Vivian Fine," *International League of Women Composers Journal* (June 1992): 20.

31. Author's telephone interview with Fine, June 27, 1997.

32. *The Women in the Garden,* 8.

33. *The Women in the Garden,* 8.

34. *The Women in the Garden,* 14.

35. *The Women in the Garden,* 17.

36. The one exception is the Tenor's first appearance. He is to be behind a scrim, seated at a table, and wearing clothes from the 1850s, *Women in the Garden* 23.

37. Author's telephone interview with Fine, May 29, 1997.

38. *The Women in the Garden,* 42.

39. *The Women in the Garden,* 42.

40. *The Women in the Garden,* 45.

41. *The Women in the Garden,* 91–92.

42. Stephanie Von Buchau, "Reports: US–San Francisco/Bay Area," *Opera News* 47 (July 1982): 34, quoted by Jones, "Solo Piano Music," 181.

43. Charles Shere, "Port Costa Players: Fine Premiere," *High Fidelity/Musical America,* June 1978, MA 20.

44. Shere, "Port Costa Players," MA 21.

45. Fine had experimented with using musical quotes to highlight the text in *The Women in the Garden.* A passage from Satie's *Three Flaccid Preludes for a Dog* is heard when Stein compares humanness and dogs, and a hint of Chopin's *Funeral*

March accompanies Isadora's passage about death. Robert Commanday mentioned this in his preview of the opera appearing in the *San Francisco Chronicle*, February 12, 1978.

46. Originally Fine wrote one *Momenti,* titled "Momento," which was published as part of a collection by friends and students of Roger Sessions in honor of his eightieth birthday *(Perspectives of New Music*, Spring-Summer 1978, 85–155).

47. Jones, "Solo Piano Music," 183–211.

48. Author's telephone interview with Fine, June 27, 1997.

49. Author's telephone interview with Fine, June 27, 1997.

50. Author's telephone interview with Fine, June 27, 1997.

51. *For a Bust of Erik Satie,* 1.

52. *For a Bust of Erik Satie,* 10.

53. This instruction is written on the score.

Chapter 6

Fulfillment

The 1980s heralded Fine's era of fulfillment, which began with several important events. First, she was elected to membership in the prestigious American Academy and Institute of Arts and Letters.[1] Then, she received a Guggenheim Fellowship, followed by a commission from the Martha Baird Rockefeller Foundation.

A number of other commissions followed. The Huntington Trio requested a piece, and Fine wrote *Music for Flute (alto flute), Oboe (English horn), and Cello* (1980). As in her recent works, she wrote interesting counterpoints that are used in retrograde, canon, exchanged amongst the instruments, and recombined in kaleidoscopic fashion. During one section motives within a line are transferred among the trio, creating a *klangfarben* coloring (see ex. 6.1). In the second measure of this example the cello has the beginning motif of a melody that the oboe introduced twelve measures earlier. The flute continues the melody in the next measure, and in the final measure the oboe completes it. Layered with this *klangfarben* variation is another exchange. The oboe in measure 2 has a line played by the cello in measures 52–54 that was originally introduced by the flute in measures 31–35. However, now it is enhanced with a 6:4 polyrhythm while the flute articulates another rhythmic version of its beginning three pitches. The cello performs a similar function in measures 3 and 4. Changes in tempo create sections that often introduce new material while recycling a line heard previously, frequently with changed rhythms and or registers. One unusual aspect is that some lines are transposed, a rarity in Fine's music. *Music for Flute (alto flute), Oboe (English horn), and Cello* ends with a retrograde canon, showing, once again, that a well-shaped line is worth hearing more than once and works well forward and backward.

The Anna Crusis Women's Choir at Philadelphia also wanted a composition. *Oda a las Ranas (Ode to Frogs)* (1980), using a poem by Pablo Neruda, resulted. Fine divided the women's choir into four parts and chose a simple instrumentation of flute, oboe, and cello with a colorful

Example 6.1. *Klangfarben* motives and reuse of material in *Music for Flute (alto flute), Oboe (English horn), and Cello* (1980).

array of percussion using ratchets, gongs, cymbals, castanets, and vibraphone. The vibraphone provides pitch support, and at one point in *Oda a las Ranas* the voices are asked to match the vibraphone timbre.[2] Like she did in the nightingale texts in previous music, Fine enjoyed writing froglike text painting, using quivering figures and doubly dotted rhythms to portray the text and having the cello add percussive textures of snapped and glissandi pizzicati. Frequently the voices are doubled by the instruments, making *Oda a las Ranas* accessible (see ex. 6.2).

During the fall of 1980 Fine completed another commission, *Trio for Violin, Cello and Piano* (1980) for the Mirecourt Trio. She wrote a large, complex, and demanding piece of two movements that are divided into sections. The movements are about equal in length, making the design symmetrical, and having a formal plan of ABC AB'D. Movement one's

Example 6.2. Text painting in *Oda a las Ranas* (1980).

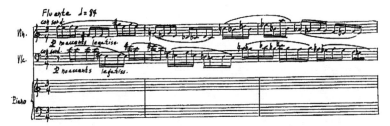

Example 6.3. Beginning measures of *Trio for Violin, Cello and Piano* (1980).
(Copyright © 1985 by GunMar Music, Inc.; used with permission.)

A section begins with a sixteenth-note canon between the violin and cello
lasting nine measures (see ex. 6.3). When composing the original line,
Fine was careful not to repeat patterns, and a few places where she did
are disguised with changes in phrasing. Similar to the opening of *Teisho*,
the pitches from this original background texture are reused throughout
the *Trio*. The B section presents "pesante e marcato" lines set in textures
that repeat and recombine, while C is a passacaglia in memory of Gregor
Piatigorsky, who died in 1976. The eight-measure passacaglia theme is
repeated eight times in a series of growing complexities. In the third repetition the violin presents the theme, expanding its register with com-
pound intervals while the cello plays the theme's retrograde (see ex. 6.4).
Further manipulations include the theme in retrograde inversion transposed down a minor third. The second movement's A section begins with
a piano texture derived from the *Trio*'s opening canon (see exs. 6.3 and
6.5) and uses similar material as the initial A, with movement two's A
enhanced with rescoring, added counterpoints, and canons. The B
section is not an exact repetition, due to rearrangements and omissions.
It is enlarged because the majority of the section is presented in retrograde. D is an elegy on a theme by Ravel paralleling the earlier passacaglia. However, the elegy's theme is only repeated three times and is
less complicated.

Example 6.4. Passacaglia theme and its retrograde in *Trio for Violin, Cello and
Piano* (1980). (Copyright © 1985 by GunMar Music, Inc.; used with permission.)

Example 6.5. Beginning of the second movement of *Trio for Violin, Cello and Piano* (1980). (Copyright © 1985 by GunMar Music, Inc.; used with permission.)

During 1981 Fine had an opportunity to present a shortened version of *Women in the Garden* as *Gertrude and Virginia: a Dialogue between Gertrude Stein and Virginia Woolf, using their own words* (1981). She extracted sections featuring Stein and Woolf and scored them for a reduced ensemble of clarinet, percussion, piano, and double bass. Fine made certain she included the section in which Woolf sang "The woman composer stands where the actress stood in the time of Shakespeare."[3]

The year of 1982 brought good fortune to Fine. The San Francisco Symphony with the help of Dr. and Mrs. Ralph I. Dorfman commissioned a piece for the 1982–83 season. John Adams, who was composer-in-residence for the symphony at that time, contacted Fine about the commission, and when she asked what size orchestra would be available, he replied: "Go for broke."[4] Fine seized the opportunity and wrote for four each of the woodwinds, six horns, four trumpets, two tenor trombones, bass trombone, tuba, timpani, and large percussion section including a whip and temple blocks, piano, celesta, harp, and strings. Such a large orchestral pallet suggested a dramatic work, and Fine used five paintings by Edward Munch as her inspiration for *Drama for Orchestra* (1982), titling the movements as "I. Mid-Summer Night," "II. The Embrace," "III. Jealousy," "IV. The Scream," and "V. Two Figures by the Shore." *Drama for Orchestra* and her previous *Women in the Garden* have common characteristics. Each movement of *Drama* is like a character in an opera and has themes and textures associated with it. "Mid-Summer Night" begins with a calm and expressive oboe melody supported by sustained string chords. The five-measure phrase is repeated by the English horn. A direct repetition is unusual for Fine, but soon this peaceful melody is disturbed by trumpet sforzando attacks resembling screams (see ex. 6.6). Later elements, such as trilled woodwinds chords, tremolo string lines, and large fused orchestral chords suggest an ominous mood that counterpoints what seems to be a lyric first movement.

Example 6.6. Lyric melody and trumpet disturbance in "Mid-Summer Night" from *Drama for Orchestra* (1982).

"The Embrace" continues the lyrical mood with a graceful melody of a descending fourth followed by a descending curve, two leaps of a seventh, and another descending curve (see ex. 6.7). This shape is important since the melody is heard immediately in inversion, creating a melodic embrace, and appears later in retrograde, retrograde inversion, and five- and six-voice canons, creating a web. However, like movement one, "The Embrace" has a disturbing foreign element. Woodwind thirds from "Mid-Summer Night" are superimposed upon "The Embrace" melody, and later a loud percussive whip sound followed by snapped pizzicato from the low strings add a sinister quality.

"Jealousy" continues this quality with a macabre scherzo in a 5/8 me-

Example 6.7. The beginning measures of "The Embrace" from *Drama for Orchestra* (1982).

ter except for a short B section, which is in 2/4. Canons, inversions, and retrogrades maintain the haunting mood.

Finally "The Scream," a sound that was introduced in the beginning of *Drama,* is the subject of movement four. High register woodwinds, fused ensemble dissonant chords, and quarter-tone brass punctuations are sonic realizations of this famous painting. Again, several kinds of canons are used, such as four-voice prolations, retrogrades, and permutations.

"Two Figures by the Shore" begins with an ostinato derived from an altered rhythmic version of the "Jealousy" theme, and superimposed thirds from movement one, which were an interruption in "The Embrace." Like in Fine's opera, characters from *Drama*'s other movements are heard as counterpoints to the ostinato. "Mid-Summer Night's" opening oboe theme, "The Embrace" melody, "The Scream's" permutation canon, and a return to "Jealousy's" original 5/8 theme appear in this finale. It would be difficult to identify this material on first hearing; however, what Fine accomplished was an internal unity. Orchestrations ranging from solo lines, doublings, and fused ensemble chords create a clarity that makes *Drama* successful. It was premièred on January 5, 1983, by the San Francisco Symphony conducted by Edo DeWaart.[5] *Drama* was so well received that the San Francisco Symphony submitted it for the 1983 Pulitzer Prize. *Drama* was the runner-up.[6]

In comparing *Drama* to *Concertante,* Fine's earlier orchestral work, one hears the ease and expressiveness of her mature writing, and although compositional complexities, such as retrogrades, inversions, and so on, exist in *Drama,* they are not substitutes for creativity but, rather, a means of maintaining internal unity.

In the fall of 1982 Fine was delighted to perform Ruth Crawford's *Sonata for Violin and Piano* (1926) with Ida Kavafian at the Coolidge Auditorium in the Library of Congress. Fine had the only surviving manuscript *of the Sonate,* considered to be a lost score, one Crawford had given her years before. Later Fine and Kavafian recorded the *Sonata* for Composers Recordings Incorporated (CRI 508) and performed it at the Kennedy Center, in San Francisco, and in New York City.

Double Variations for piano solo (1982) was composed the same year and has similar characteristics of clarity within complexity that were used in *Drama.* Pianist Claudia Stevens commissioned the work in honor of Elliott Carter's seventy-fifth birthday and premièred it at Carnegie Recital Hall on December 5, 1983. Fine was sixty-nine. The *Double Variations* is Fine's most complex piece, and in conversation with Jones, Fine commented: "The two-theme format of *Double Variations* refers to Carter's String Quartet [1951]. There is a dialogue element to *Double Variations* and it is extremely difficult. I've never played it."[7] Jones demonstrated how Fine divided the first theme into sixteen pitch groupings distributed between two voices. The groupings are further emphasized by a specific pedaling pattern, which Fine notates as a third system on the score (see ex. 6.8, part of the theme that contains pitch groupings 1–11).[8] There are nine variations; each is quite short, usually about thirty seconds, so that the listener must pay strict attention. Like Webern's miniatures, every note is significant—nothing is superfluous. Each variation features one special aspect. Variation two is identical to variation one but in invertible counterpoint; variation three is monophonic; four is a scherzo with the theme in dyads; five introduces theme two in five-note groupings while theme one continues its dyads (see ex. 6.9); six is a canon using fragments of both themes; seven is theme one in augmentation accompanied by theme two; eight is theme two in dyads; and the con-

Example 6.8. Beginning measures of *Double Variations* for piano solo (1982).

Example 6.9. Beginning measures of variation five in *Double Variations* for piano solo (1982).

cluding section is marked "fugato." *Double Variations* are a tour de force in Fine's catalog. Looking back at her early *Four Polyphonic Pieces for Piano,* which she premièred at Yaddo in 1932, and comparing it to the *Double Variations,* one notices her development as a composer. Never has she comfortably produced the same kind of composition over and over, but, instead, Fine continues to explore new ideas using her own free musical voice not hampered by any preconceived system.

The next entry in her catalog, *Canticles for Jerusalem* for voice and piano (1983), reflects the ominous and disturbing elements of *Drama,* which are achieved through similar compositional procedures of recycling material. Fine titles the *Canticles* a song cycle, a new term for her. There are five songs using various Hebrew texts in translations, but together they form a whole, with the first song, "My heart's in the East," describing the desire to return to Jerusalem. The song begins with an unaccompanied melismatic vocal phrase whose head motif, C-B♭-G♭ (see ex. 6.10), and other pitches are reused in this and later songs. The piano provides the unity and dramatic expression for the cycle. The beginning tex-

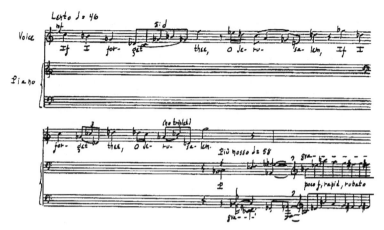

Example 6.10. Beginning measures of "My Heart's in the East" from *Canticles for Jerusalem* (1983).

tures, seen in example 6.10, are reused. The eighth-note passage is extended and heard in retrograde, and then its rhythm is changed, and it becomes a counterpoint to a quintuplet accompaniment figure. The second song, "This year I traveled far," describes the visit to Jerusalem, which is coupled with interior suffering: "but the howl I heard within is still from my Judean dessert."[9] The dyad C-B$\flat$ of the first song (see exs. 6.10 and 6.11) appears again in the second, but is transformed into a berceuse figure, suggested by the text "rocking soothes a baby." This passage is used as invertible counterpoint, which extends its usefulness, and pitch groups from the vocal line of the first song and parts of the second are set to new text. The third song, "Light against the Tower of David," is marked "Joyous," which is portrayed by the accompaniment's rapid figuration. At times segments of the figuration are heard as a slower moving vocal melody. Even more unity is achieved when part of a phrase from song two, originally unaccompanied, is reset with new text and accompaniment in song three. The fourth song, "By the rivers of Babylon," is Psalm 137 and forms a contrast in the cycle. Strummed chords on the piano strings evoke the harps mentioned in the psalm. The first song's head motif, C-B$\flat$-G$\flat$, and portions of its beginning phrase are heard in the ending of song four. The final song, "Ode to Zion," is recapitulatory. Phrase segments from previous vocal lines and the accompanying dyads from example 6.10 return. A prominent melody from the last song later becomes part of a piano interlude and an ending canonic passage. Although each song is focused upon a particular expression, such as longing or light,

Example 6.11. The C-B♭ dyad and berceuse figure in "This year I traveled far" from *Canticles for Jerusalem* (1983).

Fine treated the five songs as part of a whole rather than as four or five independent songs, as in her earlier groupings.

Another song cycle soon followed, *Ode to Henry Purcell* for soprano and string quartet (1984),[10] which was funded by a commission from the Elizabeth Sprague Coolidge Foundation. Still under the influence of *Drama* and *Canticles for Jerusalem,* Fine's attention was focused upon contemplative concerns. She choose poetry from Rainer Maria Rilke's "Sonnets to Orpheus" and Gerard Manley Hopkins's "Pied Beauty" and "Henry Purcell" for her ensemble of string quartet and soprano, a combination she had used in *Four Songs* (1933) and on a larger scale in *Teisho* (1975), which was scored for string quartet, eight solo singers, and a small chorus. Her plan was to have each song followed by an "Air on a Ground," a choral-like texture for the string quartet, referencing, perhaps, Purcell's use of a ground bass as in his *Dido and Aeneas. Ode to Henry Purcell* is designed as: (1) "Sonnet to Orpheus" followed by "Air on a Ground"; (2) "Pied Beauty" followed by "Air on a Ground"; (3) "Sonnet to Orpheus"; and (4) "Henry Purcell" followed by an "Epilogue." There is no "Air" after the third song because the "Air on a Ground Bass" becomes the accompaniment for "Henry Purcell." Fine wrote counterpoint with long phrases for "Sonnet to Orpheus" (see ex. 6.12). Frequently each member of the string quartet functions as a singer, having phrase lengths and rhythmic patterns similar to Fine's vocal realization of the poetry. As was her custom, Fine composed all of the parts simultaneously,[11] so often the strings forecast or comment upon the text but rarely repeat a vocal line. Also, crucial pitches for the soprano are woven into the quartet's passages. For the most part, Fine refrained from using retrogrades, inversions, and canons, techniques to create texture and unity. However, one interesting use of her kaleidoscoping is in the first "Sonnet to Orpheus." The text is about listening as a spiritual tool for understanding, and for the closing passage "Und wo eben kaum eine Hutte war, dies zu empfangen" ("And where before there was hardly a shed where this listening could go"), Fine recapitulated the string quartet's lines by superimposing phrases from differing parts of the sonnet.

Example 6.12. Counterpoint in "Sonnet to Orpheus" from *Ode to Henry Purcell* (1984).

"Pied Beauty" begins with a vocal solo, "Glory be to God for dappled things." Fine reflects this dappling and Hopkins's creative use of language in the string quartet's accompaniment to the voice. She composed a four-measure ostinato of sextuplets and a quintuplet for the first violin, which is so variegated it is impossible to find a pattern for the multitude of pitch choices and the subtle phrasing in groups of 12, 6, 9, 7, and so on. The second violin's countermelody is formed from pitches at the end of each sextuplet. In previous compositions when Fine wanted such a texture, she would use a rotational pitch system, retrogrades, and canons, as in *Missa Brevis*. Such is not the case with "Pied Beauty." When the ostinato is repeated, it is moved to another voice and thickened by having an additional voice move at a third below and then in the next cycle by having voices a third above and below. The texture is further variegated by having a slower countermelody shift so that it outlines other pitches from the active texture (see ex. 6.13).

In the third song of the cycle, a second "Sonnet to Orpheus," Fine has the quartet's material provide unity and contrast. Its energetic four-measure phrase announces and influences the soprano's beginning solo passage. Later the quartet's phrase returns trilled and elongated to seven measures. A pizzicato ostinato texture somewhat reminiscent of "Pied Beauty" becomes the setting for a new section, which is a mixture of *sprechstimme* and normal singing. Both ideas, the phrase and the ostinato, are repeated, forming an ABAB shaped accompaniment, although the soprano melody has very little repetition.

The last song, "Henry Purcell," is simpler, with the melodic praises to Purcell embroidered upon the repeating Ground. A vocal quote from the first "Sonnet to Orpheus" ends "Henry Purcell" and leads to the epilogue,

Example 6.13. Dappling in "Pied Beauty" from *Ode to Henry Purcell* (1984).

which repeats the ostinato from Hopkins's "Pied Beauty" but with new melody and text by Rilke placed above.

Commissions and opportunities to compose for large ensembles continued to cross Fine's path. In 1984, at age seventy-one, she received funding from the Serge Koussevitsky Music Foundation to write *Poetic Fires* (1984) for piano and orchestra. It was to be premièred at Alice Tully Hall the following year by the American Composers Orchestra conducted by Gunther Schuller, and Fine would be the pianist. She returned to a favorite theme, Greek mythology, using short passages by Aeschylus and Homer containing imagery of sea waves, the appearance of a deceased mother, Sirens amidst a hedge of dead men's bones, Aeolus and hollow winds, Night, and Jove's harp. *Poetic Fires* is designed as two large movements divided into three sections, each inscribed with its associated text. The text's imagery becomes the character for that section, suggesting linear shapes and orchestration. Having just completed *Drama,* Fine chose to use a large orchestra with the woodwinds doubling on piccolo, English horn, bass clarinet, and contrabassoon and the brass section consisting of four French horns, two C trumpets, two tenor trombones, a bass trombone, and tuba. The percussion is extensive: timpani, glockenspiel, xylophone, vibraphone, temple blocks, wood blocks, ratchet, suspended cymbal, and triangle. Harp, strings, and piano complete the instrumentation. The piano is not a solo instrument as in a concerto, but a member of the orchestra whose timbre Fine mixes with other instruments and occasionally features in a solo passage. Now an experienced orchestrator, she chose to write thin contrapuntal textures of two or three voices. The phrases are short with a wide ambitus often containing her favored intervals of fourths and sevenths, and she felt much freer to write polyrhythms (sometimes including a rhythmic reduction in parenthesis), changing meters, and other rhythmic nuances for a large ensemble. In example 6.14, the bassoon is repeating a previous cello melody. Note also the interior piano sounds and the contrapuntal texture. Fine may have felt that since she knew Schuller would be the conductor, she need not be inhibited.

Poetic Fires does not stress the internal unity of *Drama,* such as the cyclic use of material and many canons. Instead, Fine experimented with

Example 6.14. Rhythmic nuances and orchestration in "The Sirens . . . sit amidst . . . a hedge . . . Of dead men's bones" from *Poetic Fires* (1984).

unusual orchestral doublings and swathes of orchestral colors. There are passages in which the glockenspiel doubles a trumpet and an English horn doubles a flute; the bassoon repeats a previous piano passage; and the section about the sirens begins with a cello solo repeated by the contra bassoon. Bassoon, xylophone, and piano are mixed during the section about Aeolus, and other unusual pairings and doublings appear. It is almost as if Fine considers the instrumental timbres to be dancers whom she features in solos and small ensembles. Although she does use some retrograde and canons, they do not structure *Poetic Fires* but generally are an opportunity to try new mixes of timbre.

Having completed such large works as *Drama for Orchestra,* the *Double Variations, Canticles for Jerusalem,* and *Poetic Fires,* Fine returned to a simpler neobaroque style for several pieces composed between 1985 and 1986. Her *A Song for St. Cecilia's Day* (1985), with the text by John Dryden, is for chorus, orchestra, soprano, and baritone and resembles a Handelian oratorio. There are beginning and closing choruses (both using the same music but different text), solo movements for the baritone and soprano, who has a da capo aria (the first time Fine had used this design), and passages for the chorus that are generally in two-voiced texture with vocal and instrumental doublings. Repeated phrases, imitation, and a predominance of thirds contribute to the neobaroque style. The orchestra is small, strings and two trumpets, making a performance quite accessible. The work was commissioned by Trinity College, Burlington, Vermont in honor of its sixtieth anniversary.

Aegean Suite (1985) for piano solo is another example of her simplified style. It was commissioned by her cousin, Timothy Fine, for his twelve-year-old daughter, Rachel.[12] Having returned from a visit to Greece, Fine wrote three short movements, "Melos," "The Blue Aegean," and "Meltemi (a strong summer wind)," which a precocious piano student would enjoy performing. There are challenging phrase shapes, asymmetrical meters, and extended trills, which add to the piece's interest. However, some of the ideas and textures used in *Aegean Suite,* especially the figuration of "Meltemi" (see ex. 6.15), appear the following year in a series of more sophisticated keyboard compositions, *Toccatas and Arias.*

Fine continued to pursue a more simplified style in *Inscriptions* for two voices and piano (1986). She chose five poems by Walt Whitman: "One's Self I Sing," "Look Down Fair Moon," "A child said, What is the grass?" "When Lilacs Last in the Dooryard Bloom'd," and "Inscription," and set the texts carefully, generally syllabic, so that the words are heard. Fine did not use word painting or other musical portrayal of the text, as in the *Two Neruda Poems* or the more recent *Canticles for Jerusalem.* Instead, textures are thin, much like *Women in the Garden,* and often the piano functions as a third singer rather than an accompanist, such as presenting a previous melody in augmentation (see ex. 6.16 and note the instruction

Example 6.15. Keyboard figuration in "Meltemi" from *Aegean Suite* (1985).

Example 6.16. Piano part presenting augmentation of vocal melody in "One's Self I Sing" from *Inscriptions* (1986).

"Deliberately"). The piano also functions as the third voice in a canon, adds counterpoint, doubles vocal lines in more difficult passages, or serves a recapitulatory function, as in the last song, "Inscription," when the piano repeats passages from the first and second songs.

Fine had her first occasion to write for harpsichord when Barbara Harbach requested a piece. The result was *Toccatas and Arias for Harpsichord* (1986), which Harbach recorded on *20th Century Harpsichord Music, Vol. II* (Gasparo GSCD-266). Naturally a baroque keyboard style was fitting for the instrument, and Fine used this as an opportunity to summarize some of

her recent compositional ideas. Her *Aegean Suite*'s final toccatalike movement, "Meltemi," is a precursor to these toccatas. She did a grouping of
short pieces (movements one, three, and five are toccatas, and movements
two and four are arias), which are unified by having the last toccata use the
same material as the first but in a canon at the half-step and sixteenth-note
apart, and Aria 2 uses the beginning pitches of Aria 1. Each movement has
inversions, transpositions (often at a third), voice exchanges, and retrogrades—all current practices. The main difference is Fine's trend to simplify and to provide aural cues that reveal these practices. For example, the
first toccata begins with rapid monophonic descending gestures and an
early interruption of a dotted eighth- and sixteenth-note figure. It reminds
the listener of the beginning pitch of E♭ and will play a crucial role when
transpositions are heard and reveal the procedure used in the penultimate
section of the toccata (see ex. 6.17). The descending line continues, and the
momentum is not disturbed until a rest occurs, announcing a repeat of
everything that has been heard but transposed up a minor third. The dotted
eighth-note pattern reinforces the G♭, the level of transposition. The next
change is an inversion, which is quite noticeable since now the gestures as-
cend, then the original line beginning on E♭ returns. The toccata ends with
a final manipulation—a rhythmic change to the dotted-note pattern signals
a transposed retrograde. Each movement ends with a retrograde.

Aria 1 is a lyric two-voice counterpoint that features invertible counterpoint and transposition down a major sixth. Fine was careful to provide
the sonic cue of a trill, which begins the second voice (see ex. 6.18). The
voice exchange and a following inversion (transposed down a minor
tenth) are quite noticeable due to the trill, which is heard again in the final
measure, the closing of a retrograde of the above inversion (see ex. 6.19).

Example 6.17. Beginning of Toccata 1 showing monophonic line of descending
gestures from *Toccatas and Arias for Harpsichord* (1986).

Example 6.18. Beginning of Aria 1 from *Toccatas and Arias for Harpsichord* (1986) showing lyric two-voice counterpoint and trill as sonic cue.

Example 6.19. Closing of Aria 1 from *Toccatas and Arias for Harpsichord* (1986) showing trill ending retrograde inversion.

The second toccata is thicker due to doubling and an alternating chordal pattern. This pattern becomes the sonic cue for inversion and invertible counterpoint.

Aria 2 has several aspects. First, there is a hesitation caused by a rest at the beginning of measure 2, which seems out of place, and several phrases later an odd rhythm of thirty-second and doubly dotted eighth-notes is presented several times, just the reverse of a standard baroque rhythmic pattern (see ex. 6.20). However there is a sonic cue—an ornamented melody of the top voice outlines the beginning pitches of Aria 1 (E♭-G♭-B♭-F♭ [E]) and also hesitates on its second repetition.

The ornament becomes the recognized signal in transpositions, invertible counterpoints, and inversions. However, the more interesting aspect is the hesitation-and-reversed-rhythmic pattern, which, in retrograde, makes much better sense since the rest comes at the end of the measure and the rhythm is the normal long-short pattern. An added aspect of enjoyment is the rolled chords that accompany the reversed rhythmic pattern. When Fine wrote the inversion, she indicated that these chords should be rolled down, rather than the usual upward motion.

The final toccata is a canon of Toccata 1, as described earlier, but with the addition of rolled chords that stop the motion, replacing the rest in the original and announcing transpositions, inversions, and so on.

Fine's compositional use of retrograde and inversion is a metaphor for her stylistic interests during the late 1980s. Her previous attention to toccatas, arias, and oratorios was a kind of retrograde, a returning to earlier music as an inspiration for recent pieces, and baroque patterns were converted to accommodate her modern dissonant language.

Example 6.20. Rest, ornament, and rhythmic pattern in Aria 2 from *Toccatas and Arias for Harpsichord* (1986).

Next, Fine chose Debussy's *Sonata for Violoncello and Piano* in D minor (1915) as an inspiration for what sounds like a late romantic interpretation in Fine's catalog. Her *Sonata for Violoncello and Piano in Homage to Claude Debussy* (1986) is a large four-movement work that bears little resemblance to Debussy's sonata. In a program note to the score, Fine indicated:

> It [her sonata] was directly inspired by a recorded performance of the Debussy *Sonata* by Benjamin Britten and Mstislav Rostropovich, which I felt penetrated the music in new and wonderful ways. My musical language is very different from Debussy's, but I sought to capture some of the textures and momentum of his sonata. The careful listener will find a brief quotation in the first movement.

It is brief, a small melodic cadential passage outlining the D Dorian at the *Cédez* from page 2 of Debussy's sonata, which happens midway in Fine's movement. The Dorian mode is masked completely by the piano accompaniment, which is a bitonal A (major and minor)-A♭ figuration (see ex. 6.21). More noticeable similarities are the lento introductions (Fine's is for solo cello whereas Debussy's begins with piano alone and then introduces a solo cello passage) and a triplet rhythmic pattern heard in Debussy's introduction, which permeates Fine's movement. Actually, the first movement of Fine's *Sonata* has more momentum than Debussy's due to her use of transposition and inversion, which occur after the midway point. An active piano accompaniment made dissonant through bitonality, frequent trilled passages in the cello, and a "Tempo guisto of eighth-note = 112" give this movement an unflagging energy. Cello

Example 6.21. Debussy quotation and bitonal accompaniment in *Sonata for Violoncello and Piano* (1986).

melodies in the Fine *Sonata* have a more expanded register and larger leaps than in Debussy's, making the inversion a more interesting shape in Fine's music than it would have been for Debussy's more confined melodies.

Fine's second movement "Elegia" (marked "Con tenerezza eighth-note = 76") is the slow movement in this four-movement sonata design, and has no parallel in Debussy's *Sonata* except that the simple accompaniment using stark thirds resembles slightly the use of thirds in the "Poco animando" from page 1 of Debussy's work. Fine continues the use of transposition and inversion, adding retrograde and voice exchange, which is especially striking when the piano states the opening cello melody while the cello has the thirds. Again, the cello's broad melodic shape retains its interest in inversion and retrograde. Fine did not provide sonic cues as to these procedures, as she did in the *Toccatas and Arias,* but what the listener does notice is the consistent emotional tenor of the movement. The elegy ends with the sobbing passage shown in example 6.22.

The third movement begins with solo cello pizzicato, a texture like Debussy's second movement, "Sérénade," but Fine does not use the pizzicato to the extent that Debussy does. She maintains a percussive character through bowed tremolos, grace notes, trills, and staccato piano passages. Also, Fine used a rondo pattern of A (measures 1–21), B (measures 22–28), A (measures 29–39), C (measures 40–54), and A with a codetta (measures 55–68). The cello and piano texture merges in the B section due to pizzicato chordal triple stops and rolled piano triads. When the second A section returns, the cello and piano switch parts, a Fine favorite, and much of the C section is a canon between both instruments.

The fourth movement is an ABA form with the second A a retrograde of the first. Fine does use a sonic cue. In the first A the piano accompaniment is tertian with some bitonality but not as much as in the first movement. By measure 16 the thirds are replaced completely by secundal figures, another of Fine's favorites. This switch is quite noticeable in

Example 6.22. Sobbing ending of "Elegia" from *Sonata for Violoncello and Piano* (1986).

hearing the retrograde. The B section does not introduce new material but changes the momentum and texture. The tempo slows from quarter-note = 84 to a lento of quarter-note = 66, and the piano and cello present the beginning cello melody in a more lyrical and contrapuntal texture, with the cello providing a countermelody to its original melody now performed by the piano.

In March 1987, Fine recycled her successful dance score from 1937, *The Race of Life,* and arranged it for violin, percussion, double bass, and piano, titling the new version *Ma's in Orbit,* which was performed April 26, 1987, at the North American New Music Festival, State University at Buffalo, New York. The music is fast paced in cabaret style, with rapidly changing movements titled after Thurber's sketches: "Race," "Cuckoo," "Spring Dance," "Night-time," "Shifting Images," "Indians," and "Finish Line." Although originally the music was for piano, Fine took the opportunity to add percussive color, including flexatone, glockenspiel, woodblock, marimba, and vibraphone. *Ma's in Orbit* is light and entertaining, and Fine's innate sense of rhythm plus her experience of composing for dance give this piece an energetic nonstop momentum that successfully combines the short movements. Later, Fine would use *Ma's in Orbit* as connecting music in her opera, *Memoirs of Uliana Rooney.*

By 1987 commissions were accumulating, and Fine decided to retire from Bennington because she needed more time to compose—she was almost seventy-four years old. The Catskill Woodwind Quintet commissioned a piece, and although Fine had never written for such an ensemble, she decided that woodwinds should dance, too (probably she had just finished *Ma's in Orbit*), and composed *Dancing Winds* (1987). The piece is in four sections, and the textures and tempi resemble a baroque dance format of slow, fast, slow, fast. She used the ensemble in several ways. The slow first movement, "Andante molto quarter-note = 54," features the quintet as a composite instrument, with long phrases created by different pairings amongst the group. Fine's recent tendency to simplify and use more consonant intervals is apparent immediately. The head motif is an ascending figure of A-F-C♯, sounding minor sixths, and other motives have tonal references. Although dissonance is present, it is not the focal point. Instead, transpositions and developmental motivic play with limited instances of retrograde are the materials for this movement. Counterpoints of spacious ascending and descending gestures, long phrases, and some exchange and reordering of material give the first section a graceful balletlike character (see ex. 6.23).

The tempo is faster and the mood becomes humorous for the second section as playful figures of neighbor-tones, repeated notes, and seventh chords rotate amongst the quintet. These shapes are inverted, transposed, and repeated as a retrograde, and, as in her *Toccatas and Arias,* Fine provided clues for the listener, such as the accent appearing at the end of the retrograde inversion patterns in example 6.24. Thin scoring, frequent doublings, and the use of two contrasting short figures give this movement an aural integrity that is easy to follow, especially when a retrograde section has the reverse action of a previous pyramid texture, with instruments dropping out instead of adding on as in the original.

The slow third section begins with a sensuous anacrusis figure that is the principle material for thirty-eight measures. Fine manipulates the anacrusis cleverly, enlarging the gesture or reducing the figure to just a grace note. It is a simple idea that works well. Each instrument varies the figure in some way. The oboe presents it on the downbeat; the bassoon extends the duration of the ending pitch; the French horn augments the duration, making a four-measure melody, and so on. Familiar material returns when the beginning of the first section is repeated, which works well since

Example 6.23. Spacious balletlike gesture in the beginning of *Dancing Winds* (1987).

Example 6.24. Reversed accents in figures from section two of *Dancing Winds* (1987).

both have the same tempo. A similar situation happens with the fast last section. New material is heard, this time as a unison melody for the quintet, with asymmetrical groupings of fives and fours in a triple meter. It becomes a retrograde with a countermelody derived from previous material in the French horn and bassoon. A slight slowing of the tempo occurs when section two returns and closes the piece. *Dancing Winds* is recorded by the Catskill Woodwind Quintet on Redwood Records.

Fine's next composition, *Toccatas and Arias for Piano* (1987), is a challenging piece that she wrote for Veda Zuponcic, a Russian pianist who premièred it at New York's Weill Recital Hall in 1989.[13] Allan Kozinn, critic for the *New York Times,* who attended the concert, wrote: "The work [*Toccatas and Arias*] requires finger power and concentration. Miss Zuponcic sailed through its thunderous explorations of the keyboard's full range with clarity and apparent ease."[14]

Although this composition has the same title as Fine's harpsichord piece written the previous year, and uses baroque figuration, inversion, retrograde, invertible counterpoint, and canons, the *Toccatas and Arias for Piano* is a different work. Jones explores it thoroughly,[15] and in comparing these *Toccatas and Arias* with recent works, one sees some similar keyboard passages in Toccata 1 to the S*onata for Violoncello and*

Example 6.25. Triads in Toccata 3 from *Toccatas and Arias for Piano* (1987).

Piano and an ascending gesture in Aria 1 that resembles a similar idea in *Dancing Winds*. A particularly interesting section is Toccata 3, which is a virtuostic use of alternating nonfunctional triads and their inversions (see ex. 6.25), something Fine would never have written earlier, but material she uses effectively in her later years. The triads allow bitonal inferences, and a simple change in texture, such as simultaneous triads, signals a retrograde and other manipulations that Fine wants the listener to recognize.

The idea of instrumental lieder still fascinated Fine, and although *Emily's Images* for flute and piano (1987) is not titled "Songs for Flute," they are small tone poems based on the titles of first lines of poems by Emily Dickinson.[16] The collection is dedicated to Jayn Rosenfeld, flutist, who with Evelyn Crochet, pianist, premièred them on September 15, 1987, in Puerto Rico. Each movement portrays one image. "A Spider sewed at Night" is a spinning flute line generally outlining half- and whole-steps with asymmetrical groupings for flexibility (see ex. 6.26). Of course, the spider imagery is obvious, and the eight-measure melody is even repeated exactly for the second half of the piece, but what is significant is that this melody generates most of the pitch material for the other movements. It becomes a pointillistic marchlike asymmetric theme for "Exultation is the going," a birdsong for "The Robin is a Gabriel" (see ex. 6.27 and note that it begins with the second measure of "A Spider sewed at Night"), a canonic texture with occasional crossing of voices for "The Leaves like Women interchange," and a spasmodic reiteration for "A Day! Help! Help! Another Day" (see ex. 6.28). The two other movements, "A Clocked stopped-Not the Mantel's" and "After great pain, a formal feeling comes," use intervals and rhythms evocative of their titles,

Example 6.26. "A Spider sewed at Night" from *Emily's Images* (1987).

Example 6.27. "The Robin is a Gabriel" from *Emily's Images* (1987).

Example 6.28. "A Day! Help! Help! Another Day" from *Emily's Images* (1987).

for example ninths and sevenths for the clock and thirds and triadic out-lines for the "formal feeling."

Fine wrote *In Memoriam: George Finckel* (1987) in honor of her deceased friend and colleague who had performed many of her compositions, and whose cello class was the inspiration for her *Missa Brevis*. It was appropriate that she chose four celli. *In Memoriam*'s form is ABBA, an unusual symmetrical shape for Fine, and the texture resembles the choral-style writing in *Missa Brevis*. The A section is a sustained adagio, while the B section has a texture change to bowed tremolos harmonics. For the repeat of the A section Fine added an expressive line resembling the "Lacrymosa (Weeping)" movement from *Missa Brevis*. The piece was premièred September 13, 1987, at Bennington College. Fine conducted an ensemble of sixteen celli.

Bennington College had a request. Elizabeth Coleman[17] was to be its new president, and Fine wrote "Light in Spring Poplars" (1987) for Coleman's installation. Stephen Sandy,[18] a Bennington poet, wrote the text, which included images of sun, light, and trees. The phrase "a populace but of one blood" represents Bennington's experimental and collegial spirit. Fine's "Light in Spring Poplars" is for mixed chorus, soprano soloist, viola soloist, and piano. The choral writing is straightforward, with Fine's usual dissonances of seconds, fourths, and large vocal leaps; however, the chorus is frequently supported by the piano, making the music accessible for a student chorus. The soprano and viola soloists add more challenging lines that are interlaced throughout the piece.

The After Dinner Opera Company of Queensboro, New York, wanted Fine to write for them, too. What resulted was *The Garden of Live Flowers* (1988), a humorous and clever setting of text from Lewis Carroll's *Alice in Wonderland* scored for soprano, tenor, baritone , and piano. Previously Fine had used other garden settings—*A Guide to the Life Expectancy of a Rose* and *Women in the Garden*—and *The Garden of Live Flowers* resembles both. Its cabaret style of piano and a vocal trio (*A Guide* was a duet), unusual text (which could easily be staged with props and movement), and humorous situation are an obvious link to *A Guide*. For example, in *The Garden of Live Flowers,* the flowers speak to Alice, saying her "face has got some sense in it though it's not a clever one!"[19] and later they report that they are safe because "It [a tree] could bark, it says Bough-wough that's why its branches are called boughs."[20] Like *Women in the Garden,* Fine wrote quasi-declamatory vocal lines to ensure clarity, paying careful attention to rhythmic inflections. Generally the vocal lines are independent from the piano, except at the beginning and end. The piano part is especially clever.

The Garden begins with a piano introduction of a strange two-voice counterpoint. Even more unusual is the entrance of the vocal trio in which the three repeat the introduction, singing letters of the alphabet (see ex. 6.29). Actually they are spelling "This time she came upon a large flower

Example 6.29. Beginning of *The Garden of Live Flowers* (1988) showing pitch material used by the piano.

bed." The same passage is repeated at the end of the piece, in case the listener wants a second chance to decode the message. However, this material becomes the basis for the piano's role, which does more than just accompany the voices; it interprets and comments upon the text, such as when the opening line of the left hand is presented later as a single melody of trilled pitches accompanying the text when the flowers tell Alice they can talk. The same material is also reused in canon, as rolled chords, in an ostinato figure, and in several retrograde passages. This creative economy adds unity to what could be a strange piece.

Five Victorian Songs for soprano, flute, clarinet, viola, and cello (1988) continues Fine's penchant for choosing strong poetry and then setting it for solo female voice accompanied by a small instrumental ensemble. It was commissioned and premièred by the Capitol Chamber Artists. Fifty-five years earlier she wrote *Four Songs* (1933) for soprano and string quartet, then *The Great Wall of China* (1947) for soprano, flute, violin, cello, and piano, followed by *The Confession* (1963) for soprano, flute, strings, and piano, the stunning *Missa Brevis for Four Cellos and Taped Voice* (1972), and the more recent *Ode to Henry Purcell* (1984), a song cycle for soprano and string quartet.

The *Five Victorian Songs* is in the same tradition of her most challenging music. The texts are by Christina Rossetti, Matthew Arnold, Gerard Manley Hopkins, William Henley, and Elizabeth Barrett Browning. Fine was careful to observe rhythmic subtleties of the texts, generally writing syllabically and aiming for vocal clarity. Her recent contrapuntal emphasis is apparent with canons, retrogrades, and vocal lines reused in accompaniments; however, there is a greater unity between the singer and instruments than before. For example, the first song of the *Five Victorian Songs* begins with a five-voice canon of which the voice is the last entry, using the text "The irresponsive silence of the land" from Rossetti's poem, *Aloof* (see ex. 6.30). Thereafter the flute generally doubles the voice, which is especially important when Fine uses retrogrades (the voice is absent because, naturally, the text does not favor retrograde action) so that the flute represents the melodic line. Other canons occur with the voice being either the last or first entry.

Each song has a unifying feature. In "Cadmus and Harmonia" by Matthew Arnold, the flute and clarinet have snakelike figures portraying Cadmus's and Harmonia's final state while the violin doubles the soprano. The cello is silent. Material is reused economically with different barrings, fragmented repetition, and rearrangement of pitches. In the other songs Fine has a previous vocal melody be an instrumental counterpoint to a new vocal line. In 1991 she scored the collection as *Four Victorian Songs* for piano and voice, thinning the canonic textures and omitting one of the poems.

Almost concurrent with the *Five Victorian Songs* was a commission by

Example 6.30. Beginning canonic measures of "Aloof" from *Five Victorian Songs* (1988).

Musica Viva of Boston to write *Asphodel* (1988) for soprano, flute, clarinet, violin, viola, cello, percussion, and piano. Fine chose William Carlos Williams's poem about the flower, asphodel. Using similar instrumentation to the previous songs, Fine intensified the vocal and instrumental unity. The soprano's opening extended melismatic phrases for the word "of" are repeated by the cello, and the soprano's next phrase, an extended "as," leads a canon between it and the viola. Vocal melodies are repeated by instruments with other lines that are retrogrades of previous material. Later the extended "as" is repeated, but in inversion, an unusual feature for Fine to use for a singer; however, it is quite successful due to the extended melisma. Later as more text is presented, Fine writes long durations and a rather narrow vocal range that are juxtaposed upon an active accompaniment that is labeled "rustling sound." The texture is maintained through retrogrades and repetitions. As *Asphodel* progresses, Fine recalls past material through her kaleidoscopic recombining.

Another group in Boston was aware of Fine's music. The Harvard University Band performed her *The Triple-Goddess* on April 22, 1989. This was the first time Fine had written for band, and she used the full resources to compose a mythic tone poem. Feminine imagery prevails. The Triple-Goddess displays herself as Night, Order, and Justice. She lives in a cave with Eros, her son, whom she conceived when the Wind laid a silver egg in her womb. Rhea, her mother, attends her. Fine includes headings in the score indicating the action being portrayed. The closing measures are labeled with the following: "Eros created earth, sky, sun, and moon, but the triple-goddess rules the universe." Fine appears to have enjoyed composing this piece and allowed her sense of humor full range.

She chose a slowly moving passacaglia for the first section, using the low brass theme to portray Night. Each time the theme repeats, it is announced by the percussion: timpani, then chimes, cymbal, and so on. As the section progresses, the Wind is heard, then Eros is hatched from an egg and sets the universe in motion. This birth and creation take three attempts, and Fine repeats the same music but with different tempi, first an andante, then slower, and then twice the speed. Eros, who "was double-sexed and having four heads, sometimes roared like a lion or a bull, sometimes hissed like a serpent or bleated like a ram," is portrayed in a cadenza of sonic effects such as glissandi trombones and bleating woodwinds. In contrast to the comic Eros, Night ends with a tonal chorale representing her triadic nature, and Rhea is portrayed by the anvil that marks the chorale's downbeats.

Fine and her husband, Ben, had a special project come to fruition in 1988—their edited collection of essays about Louis Rapkine was published.[21] Rapkine, a French scientist who rescued French and German scientists during World War II, was a distant cousin of Ben's and someone he knew during his student days in Paris. The book commemorates the fortieth anniversary of Rapkine's death and contains contributions by outstanding scientists, including Bathsheva de Rothschild (who was Rapkine's student at the Sorbonne) and Joseph Needham. Of particular interest to Fine was Rapkine's theory of aesthetics—"the life process is the reduction of entropy within a system. Man's mind wants to capture decreased entropy, to arrest time and randomness, to create illusions through his art."[22]

At about the same time, Fine was working on a project that was important to her, a quintet for string quartet and trumpet. Ida Kavafian, the violinist with whom Fine had recorded Crawford's *Violin Sonata,* asked for a piece that would be performed at Angel Fire, a summer music festival that Kavafian and others produced in New Mexico. Recently Fine had been thinking about Palestrina's *Madrigali Spirituali* and decided to use the title as a "jumping off" place.[23] Asked why she included a trumpet, her reply was "because they had one,"[24] and it plus the quartet created the five-part texture reminiscent of the Madrigals. Fine is especially fond of her *Madrigali Spirituali* because she thinks of it as having "spiritual overtones."[25]

The first section, marked Lento (there are six sections), is a series of arched antecedent and consequent phrases occurring between the trumpet and cello and later the first violin. Each acts as a solo vocalist although the timbral differences are quite marked, creating the impression of spatial antiphonal voices. Fine reported that she used some leftover material from her *Missa Brevis,* most likely lines intended for Jan DeGaetani, for the *Madrigali*'s first movement, which explains its "spiritual" aspect.[26] The movement is short, with the string quartet providing several cadences of a unison G or major third of E♭-G. Such attention to consonance is becoming more prominent in her later works. The second section continues the slowly moving unison and consonant texture using the ensemble with muted trumpet for blending purposes. Fragments from the beginning are heard, sometimes rearranged and recombined in a meditativelike setting. The third section introduces a different atmosphere, which might seem out of place for this piece but is actually techniques from previous compositions, such as string harmonics from *Missa Brevis,* trumpet half-valving to produce quartet tones heard in the *Quartet for Brass,* and a texture of rapid dynamic envelope changes also from the *Quartet* and *Missa Brevis.* Someone familiar with Fine's music would recognize these. The next section recalls another favored texture, a canon between two violins. The canon is new material, and fragments are reused later. The fifth section, an allegro, is a rescoring of material from *Asphodel* with the trumpet having the soprano line. The ending is a return to the beginning section. Fine's *Madrigali Spirituali* is a scrapbook of favorite ideas or voices from her past works that summarize some of her deepest feelings.

Fine composed two other compositions in 1989: *The Heart Disclosed,* a monodrama for voice and piano commissioned by Claudia Stevens, for which the score is missing, and *Discourse of Goatherds* (1989) for solo bass trombone. The interesting aspect of this piece is that Fine created an actual discourse. The first section, labeled "Amorous," is a collection of phrases moving rather slowly in quarter- and half-notes that are later fragmented and juxtaposed in the second section's "Boisterous," which consists of fast moving passages of eighth- and sixteenth-notes forming short phrases and figures that are interrupted frequently by passages from the previous section, creating the impression of two goatherds having a lively conversation (see ex. 6.31).

Fine's next composition, *Portal* (1990), for violin and piano, was a commission by a young violinist, Pamela Frank, as part of an Avery Fisher Grant. Since Frank was playing her debut recital at Alice Tully Hall, Fine's idea was that the piece be like a doorway or portal to this young woman's career. Not surprisingly, the structure is a large arch shape. The piece begins with a grand six-measure gesture (see ex. 6.32) that is transposed, followed by a second shorter gesture that is also transposed, and then both gestures are presented in retrograde. The B section, the middle part of the arch, has a simpler idea featuring a violin solo that the piano repeats while the violin performs a retrograde, and the C section forms the descending incline with an inverted recapitulation of measures 1–40.

Other performers were wanting Vivian Fine compositions. David Jolly, a French hornist, was performing with Eriko Sato, violinist, and Fred Sherry, cellist, as part of the festival, Chamber Music Northeast, Portland, Oregon. Fine knew Jolly and wrote *Songs and Arias* (1990) for the en-

Example 6.31. A conversation in *Discourse of Goatherds* (1989) for solo bass trombone.

Example 6.32. Beginning gesture of *Portal* (1990) for violin and piano.

semble. Illustrating Fine's interest in instrumental song form, her *Songs and Arias* is a collection of seven short movements featuring differing styles, such as Romantic, Elizabethan, operatic, classic, contemporary, baroque, and Spanish, and moods from serious to hilarious, as suggested by the following titles: "Love-Song," "Elizabethan Song," "Rupert's Aria from the opera 'Unfulfilled,'" "Arioso," "Duet," "Aria from the cantata 'Leben O süsses schreckliches Leben,'" and "Canto Hondo (Deep Song)." Each movement is short, with generally only a phrase or two to suggest the mood and style, and then is often reused in retrogrades or recombined. One exception is the second song, "Elizabethan Song," for which she rescored "Dirge" from her *Four Elizabethan Songs* (1937–41) giving the soprano line to the French horn accompanied by muted violin and cello. One of the most humorous is "Rupert's Aria"; in the penultimate measure Fine indicates in the French hornist's part that "he falls asleep."

Fine abandoned humor and maintained a serious mood for her next composition, *Songs of Love and War* (1991) for soprano, violin, oboe, bassoon, percussion, and piano, which was commissioned by the soprano Marlene Walt in memory of her husband, Stephen. This is not a cycle, but a series of songs about death using lyrics from some of Fine's favorite sources: Walt Whitman, Jozef Wittlin (translated by Joy Davidman), Emily Dickinson, and "The Song of Songs" from the Old Testament. The music is simple and at times severe, as in example 6.33, a passage from "Stabat Mater" in which a Polish mother finds her dead soldier son dangling in the air with no shoes because the Nazis had taken them. Often Fine doubled the vocal line, frequently with the oboe, and although the ensem-

Example 6.33. "Stabat Mater" from *Songs of Love and War* (1991).

ble is quite large, she refrained from overwriting, having sparse counterpoints and occasional percussive material highlight the text.

Joan Stein, the pianist who premièred *Sonata for Violoncello and Piano* (1986), commissioned *Hymns* for two pianos, French horn, and violoncello (1991). In a note to the cover page Fine wrote: "A hymn . . . originally meant a form of 'woven' or 'spun' speech. Although the etymology is not Greek but Asiatic, the word derives from a Greek word for weaving, hyphainein."[27] The idea of weaving reflects Fine's tendency to self-borrow. The first movement, "Aeolus, god of the winds," is from *Poetic Fires* and the second, "Toward a distant shore," incorporates patterning and sketches from *Drama*'s "Jealousy." Fine stated that since compositions were often only heard once, she had no objections to rewriting for different instrumentation.[28]

A similar situation occurred with *Canciones y Danzas* for flute, guitar, and cello (1991). Fine was intrigued by a request from a guitarist since she had never composed for that instrument, and the *Canciones y Danzas* is an interesting fusion between and among the three instruments as well as a " Soliloquio" for solo guitar. There are four movements: "Adios, Bilbadito (Farewell to Bilboa, 1937)," an adaption of dance music for one of Hanya Holm's dances in reaction to the Spanish Civil War; "Oda a las Ranas (Ode to Frogs) after Neruda's poem," a reworking of a previous piece for women's chorus and small ensemble; "Tango with the Frog-Prince," a humorous and effective movement in which the guitar is the Frog-Prince and the flute is "The Senorita" (see ex. 6.34); a virtuostic and impassioned seventeen-measure "Soliloquio" that repeats itself in retrograde; and "Jiga de la Muerte (Death's Jig)," a sinister dance that possibly was from her work with Holms.

In 1993 Fine made an instrumental version for flute, clarinet, percussion, piano, violin, and cello of her *Canticles for Jerusalem*, titling this version *Canticles from the Other Side of the River* and rearranging the order of the movements.

The many years of Fine's creativity and imagination coalesced in her last major work, the *Memoirs of Uliana Rooney* (1994), a multimedia chamber opera with the libretto by Sonya Friedman. In 1993 the Dallas Opera company together with grants from Meet the Composer/Reader's Digest Commissioning Program, National Endowment for the Arts, and the Lila Wallace-Reader's Digest Fund commissioned Fine to write an opera. Eager to begin this project, Fine already had an idea. In 1987 she was intrigued by John Rockwell's article "Erwin Nyiregyhazi, Dies at 84; Pianist Regained Fame in 70's."[29] A child prodigy and composer recognized by Ernst von Dohnanyi, Arnold Schoenberg, and others, Nyiregyhazi ceased performing publicly in the 1930s and wrote Hollywood film scores. Then in 1973 he played a recital of pieces he had not studied for fifty years and made sev-

Example 6.34. Humor in "Tango with the Frog-Prince" from *Canciones y Danzas* (1991).

eral CDs. Naturally Fine noticed the similarity between his early youth and hers, both child prodigies at the piano and young composers; however, what really intrigued her was the ending sentence of the obituary: "He is survived by his 10th wife, Doris." Of course there was not such a parallel in Fine's life, but then she began toying with the idea that it would be fascinating to switch genders and create a female character—a composer who has survived many husbands rather than abandon her artistic career.

When this opportunity arose to compose an opera, Fine contacted Sonya Friedman, a film writer, producer, and director who also wrote and produced the translation titles for opera on television, and in Friedman's words, "Fine handed me this obituary, saying, 'Make him a woman!' and I did."[30] This was the first time Fine worked with a librettist, and the two collaborated to create Uliana Rooney, "a fictitious, feisty, feminist American composer."[31] Being practical, Fine was thinking in terms of a chamber opera, like her *Women in the Garden,* and Friedman thought that film and slide projections could replace conventional stage sets. But Fine, now age eighty, had an additional agenda—the opera would be her memoirs; the fictitious Uliana would resemble some aspects of Vivian's life, and she would quote parts of her compositions in the opera's score.

Fine and Friedman worked closely together and cast the opera for a soprano (Uliana Rooney), two baritones (a narrator and Uliana's husbands), and a chorus of two female voices. The orchestra was a combo for flute doubling on piccolo, clarinet doubling on bass clarinet, violin, cello, double bass, piano, and percussion of one player with a multitude of instruments. The *Memoirs of Uliana Rooney* begins with its theme music, Fine's *The Race of Life,* which sets a cabaretlike atmosphere suggesting the sociopolitical operas of Kurt Weill. The music returns several times during the opera.

Friedman's libretto is divided into the following fifteen short sections with slides and film clips that establish the mood: (1) "Memoirs of Uliana Rooney—Kansas in the early 1900s"; (2) "Uliana: Girl Prodigy"; (3) "A Woman in a Musical Profession?"; (4) "Bah to the Bourgeoisie"; (5) "First Love, First Marriage"; (6) "The Great Depression"; (7) "Untitled. A section about frozen meats, fruits, and vegetables"; (8) "Uliana Becomes Mrs. Tommy Rooney"; (9) "Untitled. A conversation between Gustav and Alma Mahler"; (10) "Untitled. Doris Humphrey's and Charles Weidman's dance troupe"; (11) "World War II"; (12) "The Home Front"; (13) "The Mysteries of Love and Politics"; (14) "All God's Children"; and (15) "Love Makes the World Go Round and Round."

Uliana has five husbands who represent the different decades of her life: a painter (1920s), a union organizer (1930s), a GI named Ben (1940s), a member of the FBI (1950s), and an environmentalist (1960s). Friedman's libretto is cleverly set with sections in rhymed verse. For example, in the section about the Girl Prodigy, Uliana speaks:

> What makes a prodigy of a child?
> A gene gone wild?
> I made a fugue in my head when I was almost three.
> They didn't believe me
> 'till I played it on the ivory keys.[32]

The accompanying instrumental music is passages from Fine's *Four Polyphonic Pieces* and adaptations of Bach's *Two-Part Invention* in C major. In the next section, Gustave Kerler, a musical director of the period, sings while a harplike figure is dispersed throughout the combo:

> In orchestras, women must play only the harp,
>   seated in a ladylike position.
> A ladylike position is impossible while playing the cello.
> And ladies do not look pretty playing winds or brasses.
> Why should they spoil their good looks? . . .
> Also women cannot be depended upon on to work hard
>   or to rehearse regularly.[33]

More feminist statements continue when Uliana speaks:

> Now how do I screw up the courage to be a composer,
> amid the European
> greats, the heavyweights?
> "I have three huge handicaps:
> I'm American, I'm a woman, and I'm alive."[34]

Friedman acknowledges the quotation as Ellen Taaffe Zwilich's words, which she spoke during an interview. Zwilich was the first woman to win the Pulitzer Prize in music. Uliana sings *sprechstimme* during this section, and Fine quotes passages from Schoenberg's "Pierrot lunaire."

As Uliana's love life evolves, Fine uses the beginning measures of her *Romantic Ode for String Orchestra* as the love theme of the opera. Uliana's first husband, Boris, a self-absorbed Surrealist painter/poet, is not supportive of her work. When she announces "Good news, I sold a cantata," Boris replies "Errata, errata."[35] Tommy, the second husband, encourages Uliana when she speaks: "Times are too hard for the avant-garde. Why write music that's out of left field. I'll write for the workers, for a fair new deal." He responds: "The Feds are giving money to artists—including dames. It's your ticket to a paycheck, and maybe to fame."[36] Uliana receives her first commission "And from the U.S.A. Equal money for women artists. Never thought I'd see the day."[37] She writes songs, marches, lullabies, and hymns. However, later Tommy gets a job and wants Uliana to stop composing. Although Fine does not make it explicit, Uliana of this period resembles Ruth Crawford, who stopped writing avant-garde music and with her husband, Charles Seeger, became interested in folk music and later music for children.

Uliana does not have a role model. At the end of section 8, after divorcing her second husband and beginning to write a ballet, she speaks:

> What to look forward to? Whom to look up to?
> What condition, what tradition?
> What to look back on?[38]

Fine and Friedman provide a model. The opera's centerpiece is the section between Gustav and Alma Mahler. In a note to the score, Fine wrote: "The music for this section is freely adapted from a song by Alma Mahler. The text is derived from letters of Alma and Gustav on the eve of their marriage."[39] The now famous passage is Gustav demanding that Alma give up her composing and accept his music as hers. She is to be what he needs—a wife and not a colleague.[40] Fine cleverly arranges Alma's song so that Gustav sings parts of her melodies. Since the style is late Romantic, and much different from Fine's sparse cabaret style, this section offers dramatic and musical contrast.

Fine's *Romantic Ode* theme announces husband number three, Ben, who is killed in World War II. He is the only husband Uliana does not divorce. During this section the chorus sings:

> Women in the factories.
> Riveting! Fast!
> Women in the Orchestras.
> At last, at last.[41]

Uliana also reminds the audience that when the men returned from the war "we [women] stepped back." [42]

Husband number four, Joe, is not announced with the *Romantic Ode* theme. It turns out he discovers her FBI file and says: "The Feds gave money to artists, including dames. It was your ticket to a paycheck. Now name names!"[43]

The 1960s are introduced with a film sequence showing events of that decade: the Kennedys, flower children, and so on. There is no action on stage, and Fine uses portions from her *Teisho,* one of her more experimental compositions, to set the mood (see ex. 6.35).

The *Romantic Ode* and husband number five (Tommy Rooney, who was husband number two) return for the last section of the opera. By now Uliana is eighty-five and Tommy sings:

> Uliana, you're still the same!
> I hear your music from sunset to sunrise.

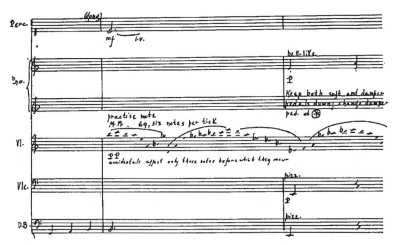

Example 6.35. A passage from *Teisho* quoted in *Memoirs of Uliana Rooney* (1994).

I even heard you even won the Pulitzer prize
So you did become all you could be,
by living for everyone,
not only for me.[44]

Fine composed the majority of melodies for her opera, making them fairly easy to sing and often adding instrumental support. Textures are thin and the main emphasis is upon hearing and understanding the text. There are no arias or passages of vocal or instrumental virtuosity. The chorus is employed minimally, and Uliana and her husbands sing duets only when it is appropriate to the text. Fine also avoided overtures, and the finale is a short chorale for all vocalists, who sing "Time can make us famous, time can make us fools, And so the best aim is to live by compassion's rule."[45] The *Memoirs of Uliana Rooney* was an opportunity for both Fine and Friedman to make a creative statement about women's issues.

A piano reduction of the opera was premièred February 1994 in New York City by the American Opera Projects Incorporated.[46] Then on September 9, 1994, a full production was given by Currents, the resident ensemble for new music at the University of Richmond, Virginia, with Fred Cohen as artistic director.

The opera is the last of Fine's compositions since both Vivian and Ben find it necessary to curtail activities in their later years. Looking back over Fine's life and catalog of music, Fine is Uliana—a strong woman who survives and thrives in spite of obstacles and nonsupportive conditions. Never has Fine taken her musical talent for granted, and although composing is a joy and comes easily, as a woman composer Fine has had to work hard. The doors of opportunity did not open as easily for her as they did for some of her male colleagues. Yet Fine has always believed in herself, her excellent ear, and her intuitive musical sense. Not succumbing to trends, yet still experimenting with new ideas, Fine has her own style. From her early strident dissonances to her wrestles with tonality, Fine's music has evolved into a freedom of expressing herself musically. She is a composer with a voice, and her life is a model to young composers who are just beginning and to older ones who might need renewing.

NOTES

1. On April 4, 1980, the *New York Times* reported that eleven new members had been elected to the American Academy and Institute of Arts and Letters. Dominick Argento was also installed at this time.

2. These directions are on page 3 of the score.

3. This appears on pages 8–9 of the score.

4. Author's telephone interview with Fine, July 11, 1997.

5. Richard Pontzious reviewed the concert for the *San Francisco Examiner,* January 6, 1983, and criticized the orchestra for a poor performance. Fine was the featured composer for the symphony's minifestival of living composers. This was the second year for such a festival; Sir Michael Tippett had been the featured composer the previous year. Fine also had an all-Fine chamber concert at the Old First Church, she spoke at the San Francisco Conservatory, and her *Four Songs* was performed by the Mostly Modern Orchestra.

6. Ellen Taaffe Zwilich won the prize that year.

7. Jones, "Solo Piano Music," 214–15.

8. Jones, "Solo Piano Music," 216.

9. Text is by Yeduda Amicah, translated by Harold Schimmel, page 8 of the score.

10. The score is supposed to be available from the Library of Congress; however, after I was informed that it was not available, I was able to obtain a copy from Adelaide Fine.

11. Author's telephone conversation with Fine, June 5, 1998.

12. Like her second cousin, Vivian, Rachel is a talented musician and became a concert pianist. Author's telephone interview with Fine, August 1, 1997.

13. Apparently, Zuponcic also made a compact disc recording of the work in Russia. Author's interview with Fine, August 1, 1997.

14. Allan Kozinn, "Concentration and Finger Power," *New York Times,* February 1, 1989. Jones, "Solo Piano Music," quotes the review on page 233.

15. Jones, "Solo Piano Music," 233–52.

16. Fine indicates this on the score that is included in the *NFA 20th-Anniversary Anthology of American Flute Music,* edited by John Solum (New York: Oxford University Press, 1993), 50–60. Some of the other composers represented in this volume are: Milton Babbitt, Emma Lou Diemer, Otto Luening, Joyce Mekeel, Mel Powell, Gunther Schuller, Joseph Schwantner, and Harvey Sollberger.

17. Little did Fine know at that time that Coleman would make sweeping changes at Bennington, including drastic changes in the music department.

18. Sandy joined the faculty in 1969, a year after Fine did.

19. *A Garden of Live Flowers,* page 3 of the score.

20. *A Garden of Live Flowers,* 6.

21. Vivian Karp and Benjamin Karp, eds., *Louis Rapkine, 1904–1948* (North Bennington, Vt.: The Orpheus Press, 1988).

22. Karp and Karp, *Louis Rapkine,* 110. These are Rothschild's words about Rapkine.

23. Author's telephone conversation with Fine, July 1,1994.

24. Author's telephone conversation with Fine, July 1, 1994.

25. Author's telephone conversation with Fine, July 1, 1994.

26. Author's telephone conversation with Fine, July 1, 1994.

27. Fine credits this as from Charles Boer, *The Homeric Hymns.*

28. Author's telephone interview with Fine, June 5, 1998.

29. *New York Times,* Thursday, April 19, 1987.

30. Notes on *Memoirs of Uliana Rooney* by Sonya Friedman.

31. Notes on *Memoirs of Uliana Rooney* by Sonya Friedman.

32. *Memoirs of Uliana Rooney,* page 3 of the libretto.

33. *Memoirs,* 54–60 of the score.

34. *Memoirs,* 65 of the score.

35. *Memoirs,* 91 of the score.

36. *Memoirs,* 109 of the score.

37. *Memoirs,* 109 of the score.

38. *Memoirs,* 121 of the score.

39. *Memoirs,* 122 of the score.

40. *Memoirs,* 134 of the score.

41. *Memoirs,* 160–62 of the score.

42. *Memoirs,* 170 of the score. The bold text is in the libretto.

43. *Memoirs,* 179 of the score.

44. *Memoirs,* 220–24 of the score. The bold text is in the libretto.

45. *Memoirs,* 237–39 of the score.

46. Grethe Barret Holby was the producer and artistic director and Miriam Charney was the pianist and music director.

Chronology

1913.   Born September 28 in Chicago.

1918.   Receives a scholarship to study piano at the Chicago Musical College.

1919–22.   Studies piano at the Chicago Musical College as a scholarship student.

1923–24.   Wins scholarship to study violin with Silvio Scionti at the American Conservatory.

1924–26.   Studies piano with Djane Lavoie-Herz.

1926.   Composes her first piece.

1926–28.   Studies harmony and composition with Ruth Crawford and counterpoint with Adolf Weidig at the American Conservatory in Chicago.

1927.   Hears Ruth Crawford's *Violin Sonata* at Cliff House Concert.

1929.   Composes *Solo for Oboe* and debuts as composer.

1930.   Composes *Four Pieces for Two Flutes; Trio in Three Movements for Violin, Viola and Violoncello;* and piece for violin and piano, which is performed at a student concert in Chicago.

1931.   Moves to New York City and is pianist at the Gluck-Sandor Dance Theater and a freelance musician for other studios; composes *Four Polyphonic Pieces for Piano; Four Pieces for Violin and Oboe* (a version of *Four Pieces for Two Flutes*) is performed at a concert of Music by Women at Hamburg, Germany, in which Fine and Crawford are the American representatives.

1932.   Becomes member of the Young Composers' Group; premières *Four Polyphonic Pieces for Piano* on April 30 at the First Yaddo Festival of contemporary American music.

1933.   Composes *Four Songs,* which is published in *New Music;* Young Composers' Group has a concert on January 15; three songs of the *Four Songs* are performed at the League of Composers concert on February 5 at the French Institute.

1934–42. Studies composition, counterpoint, and orchestration with Roger Sessions.

1935. Marries Benjamin Karp on April 5.

1937. Composes *The Race of Life* for Doris Humphrey and *Prelude for String Quartet;* hosts first formal meeting of the American Composers Alliance on December 19.

1937–45. Studies piano with Abby Whiteside; begins a more consonant style of writing.

1938. Composes *The Passionate Shepherd; The Race of Life* premières in New York on January 23; begins *Four Elizabethan Songs* (1938–41) and premières *Opus 51*, written for Charles Weidman, on August 6 at the Bennington Dance Festival; stops working as a dance accompanist; *Opus 51* is performed November 27 at the Guild Theatre in New York City and December 28 at Washington Irving High School; attends Yaddo Festivals in August.

1939. Begins *Five Preludes* (1939–41) and composes *Sonatina for Oboe and Piano; The Race of Life* is performed January 9 and 23 at the Guild Theater, January 29 at the Y.M.H.A., and January 30 at the Nora Bayes Theater; composes *Suite in E flat;* premières *They Too Are Exiles,* written for Hanya Holm, which is taken on a transcontinental tour; *Tragic Exodus,* also written for Holm, is performed February 19 at the Guild Theater and March 18 and November 25 at Washington Irving High School.

1940. Premières *Suite in E flat* and *Three Pieces for Violin and Piano; The Race of Life* is performed at Washington Irving High School on January 6, 1940; *Tragic Exodus* is performed at the Adelphi Theatre on January 7, 1940; *Tragic Exodus* and *They Too Are Exiles* are performed at the Y.M.H.A. on April 7 and Washington Irving High School on April 13; composes *Suite for Violin.*

1941. Composes music for play "Dollars and Cents."

1942. Birth of first daughter, Margaret; performance of *Opus 51* on January 17 at the Humphrey-Weidman Studio in New York City.

1943. Studies orchestration with George Szell; revival of *Tragic Exodus* with performance at the Mansfield Theater on March 17; receives an award from the Music Guild of Philadelphia for *Suite for Oboe.*

1944. Composes *Concertante for Piano and Orchestra.*

1945–48. Becomes faculty member in the piano department of New York University.

1946.	Premières *Capriccio for Oboe and String Trio; Violin Suite* is performed by the Forum Group of the I.S.C.M.
1947.	Composes *Chaconne* for piano and *The Great Wall of China,* which is published in *New Music.*
1948.	Teaches literature and materials as an adjunct faculty member of the Juilliard School; birth of second daughter, Nina.
1949.	Family moves to upstate New Paltz, New York.
1951.	Premières *Divertimento for Violoncello and Percussion;* teaches composition in summer session at the State University Teachers' College at Potsdam, New York.
1952.	Composes *Sinfonia and Fugato;* premières *Sonata for Violin and Piano.*
1953.	Composes *Variations for Harp.*
1953–60.	Serves as director of the Rothschild Foundation.
1955.	Premières *Variations for Harp.*
1956.	Receives first commission from the Rothschild Foundation and writes *A Guide to the Life Expectancy of a Rose,* which premières in New York on May 16.
1957.	Composes and premières *String Quartet.*
1958.	Articles by Wallingford Riegger and Doris Humphrey about Fine in the *Bulletin of the American Composers Alliance.*
1959.	Composes and premières *Valedictions.*
1960.	Composes and premières *Alcestis,* written for Martha Graham, on April 29 and May 8 at the 54th Street Theatre.
1961.	Composes *Duo for Flute and Viola;* begins four-year term as vice president of the American Composers Alliance.
1962.	Premières *Duo for Flute and Viola;* composes *Fantasy for Cello and Piano* and *Morning.*
1963.	Composes and premières *The Confession;* faculty member of the Connecticut College School of Dance (1963–64); teaches composition for the dance.
1964.	Composes and premières *Melos;* composes *Song of Persephone for Solo Viola* and *Dreamscape;* becomes a faculty member at Bennington College, where she teaches piano and composition.
1965.	Composes and premières *Concertino for Piano and Percussion Ensemble;* composes and premières *My Song, My Enemy* for Jose Limon August 14 at the Connecticut College American Dance Festival, New London, Connecticut; begins period of lecture-recitalist (1965–68) at Notre Dame, Wisconsin at Oshkosh, Bard College, and William and Mary.
1966.	Composes *Chamber Concerto for Cello and Six Instruments* and *Four Piano Pieces;* receives the Dollard Award.

1967.   Composes and premières *My Sledge and Hammer Ly Reclined* and *Quintet for Trumpet String Trio, and Harp.*

1968.   Jacob Glick premières the *Song of Persephone for Solo Viola* August 5, 1968, at Lenox, Massachusetts.

1969.   Composes *Paean.*

1970.   Receives Ford Foundation Grant in the Humanities; premières *Fantasy for Cello and Piano* and *Paean.*

1971.   Composes and premières *Two Neruda Poems* and *Sounds of the Nightingale.*

1972.   Composes *Concerto for Piano Strings and Percussion (One Performer)* and *Missa Brevis for Four Cellos and Taped Voice.*

1973.   Composes *The Second Prophet Bird* (also known as *The Flicker*); *Paean, Alcestis,* and *Concertante for Piano and Orchestra* are broadcast on WNYC on March 11; premières *Missa Brevis* and *Concerto for Piano Strings and Percussion (One Performer)* at an all-Fine program at the Finch College Concert Hall, New York City on April 15; premières *Morning.*

1974.   Premières *The Second Prophet Bird;* New York Public Library honors Fine with "Vivian Fine and Five Dancers," an exhibit of her manuscripts of dance compositions; receives a National Endowment for the Arts Grant.

1975.   Composes *Teisho* and *Meeting for Equal Rights 1866;* premières *The Passionate Shepherd to His Love and Her Reply.*

1976.   Composes and premières *Sonnets for Baritone and Orchestra* and *Romantic Ode for String Orchestra with solo violin, viola, and cello;* premières *Meeting for Equal Rights 1866;* composer-in-residence at Skidmore College, Saratoga, New York; receives a second National Endowment for the Arts Grant.

1977.   Premières *Teisho* (also known as *Three Buddhist Evocations*); receives funding from the National Endowment for the Arts to write *Women in the Garden.*

1978.   Composes *Quartet for Brass;* premières *Women in the Garden* and *Momenti.*

1979.   Premières *Chamber Concerto for Cello and Six Instruments* and *Quartet for Brass;* composes and premières *For a Bust of Erik Satie* and *Nightingales-Motet for Six Instruments;* composes *Lieder for Viola and Piano;* wins the Music Awards Program sponsored by the American Academy and Institute of Arts and Letters.

1980.   Premières *Lieder for Viola and Piano;* composes *Oda a las Ranas* and *Trio for Violin, Cello and Piano;* composes and premières *Music for Flute (alto flute), Oboe (English horn) and Cello;* guest at the Composers' Forum, University of Illinois, Champaign-Urbana on January 28; receives a Guggenheim Fellowship; is elected to the American Academy and Institute of Arts and Letters; receives a commission from the Martha Baird Rockefeller Foundation.

1981.   Premières *Oda a las Ranas* and *Trio for Violin, Cello and Piano;* composes and premières *Gertrude and Virginia;* receives grant from the Alice B. Ditson Foundation.

1982.   Performs Ruth Crawford's *Sonata for Violin and Piano* with Ida Kavafian at the Coolidge Auditorium in the Library of Congress on November 12; composes *Drama for Orchestra* and *Double Variations.*

1983.   Composes *Canticles for Jerusalem;* premières *Drama for Orchestra* and *Double Variations; Drama for Orchestra* is nominated for the Pulitzer Prize.

1984.   Composes *Ode to Henry Purcell;* composes and premières *Quintet for Violin, Oboe, Clarinet, Cello and Piano;* receives funding from the Koussevitsky Foundation to write *Poetic Fires.*

1985.   Premières *Poetic Fires* and *Ode to Henry Purcell;* composes and premières *A Song for St. Cecilia's Day;* composes *Aegean Suite.*

1986.   Composes *Inscriptions, Toccatas and Arias for Harpsichord,* and *Sonata for Violoncello and Piano.*

1987.   Premières *Inscriptions, Toccatas and Arias,* and *Ma's in Orbit;* composes and premières *Emily's Images, Dancing Winds, In Memoriam: George Finckel,* and "Light in Spring Poplars"; composes *Toccatas and Arias for Piano* and *After the Tradition;* retires from Bennington College.

1988.   Premières *After the Tradition;* receives a commission from the Bay Area Women's Philharmonic to write a piece in honor of her seventy-fifth birthday; composes and premières *The Garden of Live Flowers* and *Five Victorian Songs;* composes *Asphodel* and *The Triple-Goddess;* together with her husband, Benjamin Karp, edits and publishes a collection of essays about Louis Rapkine.

1989.   Premières *Canticles for Jerusalem, Asphodel,* and *The Triple-Goddess;* composes and premières *Discourse of Goatherds;* composes *Madrigali Spirituali* and *The Heart Disclosed.*

1990.   Premières *Madrigali Spirituali* and *The Heart Disclosed.* Composes and premières *Portal* and *Songs and Arias.*

1991.   Composes *Songs of Love and War, Hymns,* and *Canciones y Danzas.*

1993.   Commissioned by the Dallas Opera to compose an opera.

1994.   Completes and premières *Memoirs of Uliana Rooney* in New York City by the American Opera Projects Incorporated and given a full production on September 9 by Currents, the resident ensemble for new music at the University of Richmond, Virginia; commemorative concert in honor of Fine's eighty-first birthday performed by the Catskill Conservatory at Weill Recital Hall of Carnegie Hall, October 9.

Catalog of Compositions

VOCAL COMPOSITIONS

1933   *Four Songs*. Texts by Sixteenth-Century Anonymous, Robert Herrick, and James Joyce. Soprano and string quartet. Published by *New Music*. ©1933 by Vivian Fine. Premièred February 5, 1933, by The League of Composers. Reviewed by *New York Times*, February 6, 1933, and Theodore Chanler, "All-American," *Modern Music*, March/April 1933, 160–62. Analyzed by William Treat Upton in "Aspects of the Modern Art-Song,"*Musical Quarterly*, January 1938, 11–30.

1933–41   *Five Songs*. Texts by Emily Dickinson, James Joyce, anonymous, John Keats, and Walt Whitman. Low or medium voice and piano.

1937–40   *Four Elizabethan Songs*. Texts by John Donne, John Lyly, Shakespeare, and Philip Sidney. Medium high or medium voice and piano. Premièred May 1, 1940, at the Composer's Forum Laboratory, New York City.

1939   *Tragic Exodus*. Vocalize for baritone and piano.

1941   "Epigram" and "Epitaph: Upon the Death of Sir Albert Morton's Wife." Text by Sir William Jones and Henry Wotton. Contralto and piano.

1943   *Songs of Our Time*. Texts by Jozef Wittlin and Bertolt Brecht, translated by Joy Davidman. Medium high or medium voice and piano.

1947   *The Great Wall of China*. Text by Franz Kafka. Soprano, flute, violin, cello, and piano. ©1948 by *New Music*. Premièred May 1948 on the Alice Ditson Fund Concert at the Macmillan Theater, New York City.

1956   *A Guide to the Life Expectancy of a Rose*. Text by S. R. Tilley. Soprano, tenor, and chamber ensemble. Premièred May 16 by Bethany Beardslee, soprano, Earl Rogers, tenor, and Jacques Monod, conductor, New York City. Commissioned by the B. de Rothschild Foundation. Reviewed by Ross Parmenter in "Music: A New Concert Giving Group," *New York Times,* May 16, 1956

1959   *Valedictions.* Text by John Donne. Soprano, tenor, chorus, and ten instruments. Premièred May 1959 by the Schola Cantorum conducted by Hugh Ross, New York City.

1963   *The Confession.* Text by Jean Racine. Soprano, flute, strings, piano. Premièred March 21, 1963, New York City. Reviewed by Donal Henahan, "Concert: Music by Vivian Fine Performed at Finch," *New York Times,* April 17, 1973.

1971   *Two Neruda Poems.* Text by Pablo Neruda. Soprano and piano. Premièred December 1, 1971, by Jan DeGaetani at Bennington College, Vermont. Performed January 12, 1983, at Old First Church, San Francisco. Reviewed by Donal Henahan, "Concert: Music by Vivian Fine Performed at Finch," *New York Times,* April 17, 1973, and Heuwell Tircuit, "A Survey of Vivian Fine's Chamber Music Career," *San Francisco Chronicle,* January 11, 1983.

1972   *Missa Brevis for Four Cellos and Taped Voice.* Premièred April 15, 1973, at New York City. Performed October 2, 1990, at a Composers Incorporate concert in the Veterans Building, San Francisco. Recorded by Jan DeGaetani, mezzosoprano, and Erick Bartlett, David Finckel, Michael Finckel, and Maxine Neuman, cellists, CRI SD 434. Reviewed by Donal Henahan, "Concert: Music by Vivian Fine Performed at Finch," *New York Times,* April 17, 1973, and by Robert Commanday, "A Few Pearls Among New-Music Offerings," *San Francisco Chronicle,* October 4, 1990.

1975   *Teisho.* Various Zen texts. Singer, chorus, strings. Premièred May 22, 1976, at Bennington College, Vermont, by the Sine Nomine Singers and the Bennington College Contemporary Quartet conducted by Vivian Fine. Funded by the National Endowment for the Arts Grant.

1976   *Sonnets for Baritone and Orchestra.* Text by Keats. Premièred December 5, 1976, at North Bennington, Vermont, by Louis Calabro conducting The Sage City Symphony. Commissioned by The Sage City Symphony.

1979   *For a Bust of Erik Satie.* Text by Georges Guy translated by Harry Mathews. Soprano, mezzo soprano, narrator, and six instruments. Premièred May 11, 1979, at Bennington College.

1981   *Gertrude and Virginia.* Text by Gertrude Stein and Virginia Woolf. Soprano, mezzo soprano, and small ensemble. Premièred June 8, 1981, at New York City.

1983   *Canticles for Jerusalem,* a song cycle for mezzo soprano and piano. Texts by Judah Halevi, translated by Robert Alter and T. Carmi, and Yehuda Amichai, translated by Harold Schimmel. Performed on April 16, 1989, at Paine Hall, Harvard University, Cambridge, Massachusetts. Commissioned by Stephanie Friedman and Lois Brandynne.

1984   *Ode to Henry Purcell,* a song cycle for soprano and string quartet. Text by Gerard Manley Hopkins. Premièred October 30, 1985, by Phyliss Bryn-Julson and the Atlantic Quartet at the Library of Congress, Washington, D.C. Commissioned by the Elizabeth Sprague Coolidge Foundation. Manuscript is at the Library of Congress.

1985   *A Song for St. Cecilia's Day* for mixed chorus, soprano, and baritone soloists, string orchestra, and trumpets. Text by John Dryden. Premièred October 25, 1985, by the Trinity College chorus, the Bennington College chorus, the University of Vermont chorus, and the Vermont Symphony conducted by Vivian Fine. Commissioned by and dedicated to Trinity College, Burlington, Vermont, in honor of the sixtieth year of founding of Trinity College by the Sisters of Mercy.

1986   *Inscriptions* for two voices and piano. Text by Walt Whitman. Premièred January 8, 1987, by Nan Nall and Lise Messier, sopranos, and Flenn Parker, pianist, at Boston, Massachusetts.

        Sheila's Song for voice, piano and double bass.

1987   *The Human Mind* for voice and piano.

        "Light in Spring Poplars" for mixed chorus, soprano, solo, viola solo, and piano. Text by Stephen Sandy. Premièred October 11, 1987, on the occasion of the installation of Elizabeth Coleman as president of Bennington College. Janet Gilespie, soprano, Jacob Glick, violist, Mary Ann Finckel, pianist, and Randall Neale, conductor.

1988   *The Garden of Live Flowers* for soprano, tenor, baritone, and piano. Text by Lewis Carroll. Premièred March 27, 1988, by the After Dinner Opera Company at Queensboro Community College, New York.

        Five Victorian Songs for soprano, flute, clarinet, viola, and cello. Texts by Christina Rossetti, Matthew Arnold, Gerard Manley Hopkins, William Ernest Henley, and Elizabeth Barrett Browning. Premièred March 4, 1988, by The Capitol Chamber Artists at Green Mountain College, Poultney, Vermont. Commissioned by The Capitol Chamber Artists.

        Asphodel for soprano, flute, clarinet, violin, viola, cello, per-

cussion, and piano. Text by William Carlos Williams. Premièred April 10, 1989, by Musica Viva, Maria Tegzes, soprano, and Richard Pittman, conductor, at the Kathryn Bache
Miller Theater, New York City. Commissioned by Musica
Viva of Boston.

COMPOSITIONS FOR CHORUS

1938   *The Passionate Shepherd to His Love and Her Reply.* Text
        by Christopher Marlowe. SAA
1959   *Valedictions.* Text by John Donne. Chorus, soprano, tenor,
        ten instruments. Premièred May 1959 by the Schola Canto-
        rum conducted by Hugh Ross, New York City.
1962   *Morning.* Text by Thoreau. Chorus, narrator, organ. Pre-
        mièred June 6, 1973, at Bennington, Vermont. Commis-
        sioned by the New York Society for Ethical Culture.
1967   *My Sledge and Hammer Ly Reclined.* Text from epitaphs in
        a Vermont cemetery. Mixed chorus and orchestra. Premièred
        May 26, 1967, at Bennington, Vermont, by conductor Louis
        Calabro.
1969   *Paean* for narrator-singer (baritone or tenor), women's cho-
        rus, and brass ensemble. Text by John Keats. Premièred
        April 1, 1970, at Bennington College, Vermont. Recorded by
        the Eastman Brass Ensemble and the Bennington Choral En-
        semble, CRI SD 260. Recording reviewed by Enos E. Shupp,
        Jr., *The New Records,* August 1971, 6.
1971   *Sounds of the Nightingale* for soprano, female chorale ensem-
        ble, and chamber orchestra. Premièred May 19, 1971, at Ben-
        nington College, Bennington, Vermont, Valerie Lamoree, so-
        prano. Reviewed by Heuwell Tircuit, "A Survey of Vivian
        Fine's Chamber Music Career," *San Francisco Chronicle,*
        January 11, 1983. Dedicated to the memory of Elinor Siegel.
1975   *Meeting for Equal Rights 1866.* Collected texts by various
        authors at the time of the meeting for equal rights. Mixed
        chorus, mezzo soprano, baritone, narrator, orchestra. Pre-
        mièred April 23, 1976, by the Oratorio Society of New York
        conducted by Lyndon Woodside, Cooper Union, New York
        City. Reviewed by Donal Henahan, "Oratorio Society Sings
        Equal-Rights Cantata," *New York Times,* May 22, 1976.
        Commissioned by the Cooper Union in New York City,
        funded by The National Endowment for the Arts
        Teisho. Collected texts. Eight solo singers or small chorus

and string quartet. Premièred May 22, 1976, by the Sine Nomine Singers and the Contemporary Quartet at Bennington College, Vermont. Funded by a National Endowment for the Arts Grant.

1980   *Oda a las Ranas*. Text by Pablo Neruda. Women's chorus, flute, oboe, cello, and percussion. Premièred June 13, 1981, by the Anna Crusis Women's Choir at Philadelphia. Commissioned by the Anna Crusis Women's Choir.

1985   *A Song for St. Cecilia's Day* for mixed chorus, soprano, and baritone soloists, string orchestra, and trumpets. Premièred October 25, 1985, by the Trinity College chorus, the Bennington College chorus, the University of Vermont chorus, and the Vermont Symphony conducted by Vivian Fine. Commissioned by Trinity College, Burlington, Vermont.

1987   "Light in Spring Poplars" for mixed chorus, soprano, solo, viola solo, and piano. Text by Stephen Sandy. Premièred October 11, 1987, on the occasion of the inauguration of Elizabeth Coleman as president of Bennington College. Randall Neale, conductor.

1991   *Songs of Love and War*. Texts by Walt Whitman, Jozef Wittlin (translated by Joy Davidman), Emily Dickinson, and "The Song of Songs" from the Old Testament. Soprano, violin, oboe, bassoon, percussion, and piano. Premièred August 14, 1991, by Marlene Walt, soprano, Jeannie Shames, violin, Ralph Gomberg, oboe, Stephen Walt, bassoon, Thomas Gayger, percussion, and Gilbert Kalish, piano, at the Clark Art Institute, Williamstown, Massachusetts.

COMPOSITIONS FOR A SOLO INSTRUMENT

1929   *Solo for Oboe*. Premièred April 21, 1930, by D. Denarno at the Pan-American Association of Composers Concert at Carnegie Chamber Hall, New York City. Mentioned in *New York Times,* April 22, 1930.

1931–32   *Four Polyphonic Pieces for Piano*. Premièred April 30, 1932, at the first Yaddo Festival.

1935–41   *Music for Study* for piano. Premièred May 1, 1940 (pianist unknown), at the Composers' Forum Laboratory, New York City. Numbers 1 and 2 published by E. H. Morris in *Contemporary American Piano Music.*

1939–41   *Five Preludes* for piano. Premièred December 29, 1962, by Robert Guralnick, New York City.

1940   *Suite in E Flat* for piano. Premièred on November 21, 1946, by Vivian Fine at Temple University, Pennsylvania.

1944   *Rhapsody on a Russian Folk Song* for piano. Premièred April 30, 1944, at Town Hall, New York City.

1947   *Second Solo for Oboe.*
          Chaconne for piano.

1952   *Sinfonia and Fugato* for piano. ©1958 Lawson-Gould. Premièred June 11, 1952, by Vivian Fine at the State University of New York Conference on the Fine Arts, New Paltz, New York. Recorded by Robert Helps, CRI SD 288.

1953   *Variations for Harp.* ©1965 by Lyra Music Co. Premièred April 22, 1955, at Woodstock, New York. Dedicated to Joyce Rosenfield.

1964   *Melos* for double bass. Premièred April 8, 1964, by Bertram Turetzky at Bennington College.
          Song of Persephone for Solo Viola. Premièred August 5, 1968, by Jacob Glick at Lenox, Massachusetts.

1966   *Four Piano Pieces.* Premièred April 28, 1966, by Vivian Fine at the University of Notre Dame. Manuscript is not available.

1972   *Concerto for Piano Strings and Percussion (One Performer).* Premièred April 15, 1973, at Finch College Concert Hall, New York City. Commissioned by the Woolley Fund. Reviewed by Donal Henahan, "Concert: Music by Vivian Fine Performed at Finch," *New York Times,* April 17, 1973.

1973   *The Flicker* for solo flute or piano right hand (also known as *The Second Prophet-Bird*). Published by GunMar Music, Inc., ©1983. Premièred March 7, 1974, at Mills College, Oakland, California. Performed January 12, 1983, at Old First Church, San Francisco. Reviewed by Heuwell Tircuit, "A Survey of Vivian Fine's Chamber Music Career," *San Francisco Chronicle,* January 11, 1983.

1978   *Momenti* for piano. Published by GunMar Music Inc., ©1983. Premièred March 26, 1979, at New York City. In honor of the 150th anniversary of Schubert's death and dedicated to Roger Sessions. Recorded by Lionel Nowak, pianist, CRI SD 434.

1982   *Double Variations* for piano. Premièred December 5, 1983, by Claudia Stevens at Carnegie Recital Hall, New York City. Commissioned by Claudia Stevens in honor of Elliott Carter's 75th birthday.

1985   *Aegean Suite* for piano. Commissioned by Timothy Fine for his daughter, Rachel.

1986   *Toccatas and Arias for Harpsichord.* Premièred February 9, 1987, by Barbara Harbach at State University at Buffalo, New York. Recorded by Barbara Harbach, harpsichordist,

Gasparo GSCD-266. Recording reviewed by David Claris, *Fanfare,* November-December 1990, 435–37. Composed for Barbara Harbach.

1987   *Toccatas and Arias for Piano.* Premièred January 30, 1989, by Veda Zuponcic at Weill Recital Hall, New York City. Reviewed by Allan Kozinn in "Review/Piano: Concentration and Finger Power," *New York Times,* February 1, 1989.

1989   *Discourse of Goatherds* for solo bass (or tenor) trombone. Premièred April 20, 1989, by Matthew Guilford, bass trombonist, at Northeastern University. Dedicated to Tom Everet. *The Heart Disclosed,* monodrama for voice and piano. Premièred October 6, 1990, by Claudia Stevens at the Athenaeum in Providence, Rhode Island. Commissioned by Claudia Stevens. The music is missing.

COMPOSITIONS FOR DUOS OR TRIOS

1930   *Four Pieces for Two Flutes.* Published by GunMar Music, Inc, ©1981. Premièred December 1, 1931, at the International Society of Contemporary Music's concert of music by women, Dessau, Germany.

1942   *Sonatina for Oboe and Piano.* Premièred September 7, 1942, at Buenos Aires. Also available for violin and piano or cello and piano.

1940   *Three Pieces for Violin and Piano.* Premièred April 16, 1946, in New York City by Orrea Pernel, violinist, and Beveridge Webster, pianist, at the I.S.C.M. Forum Group. Reviewed by Lou Harrison in "Forum Group Music," *New York Herald Tribune,* April 17, 1946, and Mark Schubart, "Young Composers Offer New Works Here; Present-day Writers Show to Advantage," *New York Times,* April 17, 1946.

1952   *Sonata for Violin and Piano.* Premièred December 21, 1958, by Matthew Raimondi, violinist, and Yehudi Wyner, pianist, at the Composers' Showcase Concert, New York City. Performed January 12, 1983, at Old First Church, San Francisco. Reviewed by Heuwell Tircuit, "A Survey of Vivian Fine's Chamber Music Career," *San Francisco Chronicle,* January 11, 1983.

1961   *Duo for Flute and Viola.* Published by Carl Fischer, Inc, ©1979. Premièred February 22, 1962, by Claude Monteux, flutist, and Walter Trampler, violist.

1962   *Fantasy for Cello and Piano.* Published by Carl Fischer, Inc.,

©1976. Premièred February 13, 1970, in Carnegie Recital Hall by John Thurman, cellist, and Robert Guralnick, pianist.

1965   *Concertino for Piano and Percussion Ensemble.* Premièred March 18, 1965, by the Paul Price Percussion Ensemble, Paul Price, conductor, and Vivian Fine, pianist.

1977   *Three Buddhist Evocations.* Premièred October 4, 1977, by Daniel and Machiko Kobialka at Bennington College, Vermont.

1979   *Lieder for Viola and Piano.* Published by Arsis Press. Premièred May 7, 1980, by Jacob Glick and Vivian Fine at Bennington College. Composed for Jacob Glick.

1980   *Trio for Violin, Cello and Piano.* Published by GunMar Music, Inc., ©1985. Premièred April 4, 1981, by the Mirecourt Trio at Unity Temple, Oak Park, Illinois. Performed January 12, 1983, at Old First Church, San Francisco. Reviewed by Heuwell Tircuit, "A Survey of Vivian Fine's Chamber Music Career," *San Francisco Chronicle,* January 11, 1983. Commissioned by the Mirecourt Trio.
Music for Flute (alto flute), Oboe (English horn), and Cello. Commissioned by the Huntingdon Trio.

1986   *Sonata for Violoncello and Piano.* Premièred March 13, 1988, by Maxine Neuman, cellist, and Joan Stein, pianist, at New York City.

1987   *Emily's Images* for flute and piano. Premièred September 15, 1987, by Jayn Rosenfeld, flutist, and Evelyn Crochet, pianist, in Puerto Rico.

1990   *Portal* for violin and piano. Premièred April 19, 1990, by Pamela Frank, violinist, and Wu Han, pianist, at Alice Tully Hall, New York City. Commissioned by Pamela Frank as part of an Avery Fisher Grant. Reviewed by Allan Kozinn in "Pamela Frank, a Violinist, in New York Recital Debut," *New York Times,* April 22, 1990.
Songs and Arias for French Horn, violin, and cello. Premièred July 12, 1990, by David Jolley, hornist, Eriko Sato, violinist, and Fred Sherry, cellist, at Chamber Music Northeast, Portland, Oregon.

1991   *Canciones y Danzas* for flute, guitar, and cello.

COMPOSITIONS FOR STRINGS

1930   *Trio in Three Movements for Violin, Viola and Violincello.* Premièred November 23, 1953, by the Herrmann Trio at Darmstadt.

1933   *Four Songs.* Texts by Sixteenth-Century Anonymous, Robert Herrick, and James Joyce. Soprano and string quartet. ©1933 by Vivian Fine and published by *New Music*. Premièred February 5, 1933, by The League of Composers.

1937   *Piece for Muted Strings (Elegiac Song)* and *Prelude for String Quartet*. Premièred March 26, 1939, by the League of Composers.

1939   *Sonatina for Oboe and Piano*. Premièred September 7, 1942, at Buenos Aires. Can also be performed as violin and piano or cello and piano.

1940   *Three Pieces for Violin and Piano*. Premièred April 16, 1946, in New York City by Orrea Pernel, violinist, and Beveridge Webster, pianist, for the I.S.C.M. Forum Group.

1946   *Capriccio for Oboe and String Trio*. Premièred on April 17, 1948, by Lois Wann, oboist for the I.S.C.M. Forum Group.

1951   *Divertimento for Violoncello and Percussion*. Premièred August 19, 1962, at the Hudson Valley Philharmonic Chamber Music concerts, Storm King Art Center, New York.

1952   *Sonata for Violin and Piano*. Premièred December 21, 1958, by Matthew Raimondi, violinist, and Yehudi Wyner, pianist, at the Composers' Showcase Concert, New York City.

1957   *String Quartet*. Premièred November 21, 1957, by the Claremont String Quartet, Vassar College.

1961   *Duo for Flute and Viola*. Published by Carl Fischer Facsimile Edition, ©1976. Premièred February 22, 1962, by Claude Monteux, flutist, and Walter Trampler, violist.

1962   *Fantasy for Cello and Piano*. Premièred February 13, 1970, New York City.

1966   *Chamber Concerto for Cello and Six Instruments*. Premièred December 5, 1979, by George Finckel, cellist, at Windham College, Vermont.

1967   *Quintet for Trumpet, String Trio, and Harp*. Premièred June 3, 1967, at Washington, Connecticut. Commissioned by the Wykeham Rise School.

1972   *Missa Brevis for Four Cellos and Taped Voice*. Premièred April 15, 1973, at New York City. Recorded by Jan DeGaetani, mezzo-soprano, and Erick Bartlett, David Finckel, Michael Finckel, and Maxine Neuman, cellists, CRI SD 434.

1975   *Teisho* for eight solo singers or a small chorus and string quartet. Premièred May 22, 1976, by the Sine Nomine Singers at Bennington College, Vermont. Funded by a National Endowment for the Arts Grant.

1976   *Romantic Ode for String Orchestra with solo violin, viola, and cello*. ©1981 by GunMar Music, Inc. Premièred August 28, 1976, by conductor G. Grossman at Bennington College, Vermont. Commissioned by The Chamber Music Conference of the East.

1977   *Three Buddhist Evocations* (also known as *Teisho*). Pre-
        mièred October 4, 1977, by Daniel and Machiko Kobialka at
        Bennington College, Vermont. Performed January 12, 1983,
        at Old First Church, San Francisco. Reviewed by Heuwell
        Tircuit, "A Survey of Vivian Fine's Chamber Music Career,"
        San Francisco Chronicle, January 11, 1983.

1984   *Quintet (after paintings by Edvard Munch)* for oboe, clarinet,
        violin, violoncello, and piano. Published by Henmar Press,
        ©1985. Premièred July 29, 1984, at Chicago, Illinois. Com-
        missioned by Sigma Alpha Iota.

1986   *Sonata for Violoncello and Piano.* Premièred March 13,
        1988, by Maxine Neuman, cellist, and Joan Stein, pianist, at
        New York City.

1987   *In Memoriam: George Finckel* for four cellos or multiples
        thereof. Premièred September 13, 1987, by an ensemble of
        sixteen celli conducted by Vivian Fine at Bennington Col-
        lege, Vermont.

1989   *Madrigali Spirituali* for trumpet and string quartet. Pre-
        mièred August 27, 1989, by Stephen Burns, trumpet, Ida
        Kavafian, Pamela French, violinists, Toby Appel, violist, and
        Warren Lash, cellist, at Angel Fire, New Mexico.

1990   *Portal* for violin and piano. Premièred April 19, 1990, by
        Pamela Frank, violinist, and Wu Han, pianist, at Alice Tully
        Hall, New York City. Commissioned by Pamela Frank.
        Songs and Arias for French horn, violin, and cello. Premièred
        July 12, 1990, by David Jolley, hornist, Eriko Sato, violinist,
        and Fred Serry, cellist, at Chamber Music Northeast, Port-
        land, Oregon.

1991   *Hymns* for two pianos, French horn, and violoncello.

1993   *Canticles from the Other Side of the River* for flute, clarinet,
        percussion, piano, violin, and cello.

COMPOSITIONS FOR BRASS

1969   *Paean* for narrator-singer (baritone or tenor), women's cho-
        rus, and brass ensemble. Text by Keats. Premièred April 1,
        1970, at Bennington College, Vermont. Recorded by the
        Eastman Brass Ensemble, CRISD 260.

1978   *Quartet for Brass* for two trumpets, horn, and bass trombone.
        © 1985 GunMar Music Inc. Premièred May 22, 1979, by the
        Metropolitan Brass Quartet, New York City. Recorded by
        Ronald K. Anderson and Allan Dean, trumpeters, David Jol-
        ley, French hornist, and Lawrence Benz, bass trombonist, CRI
        SD 434. Commissioned by the Metropolitan Brass Quartet.

1988   *The Triple-Goddess* for concert band. Premièred April 22, 1989, by the Harvard University Band, Thomas Everett, conductor at the Sander Theater, Cambridge, Massachusetts.

1989   *Madrigali Spirituali* for trumpet and string quartet. Premièred August 27, 1989, by Stephen Burns, trumpet, Ida Kavafian, Pamela French, violinists, Toby Appel, violist, Warren Lash, cellist, and Stephen Burns, trumpeter, at Angel Fire, New Mexico.

1991   *Hymns* for two pianos, French horn, and violoncello.

COMPOSITIONS FOR CHAMBER ENSEMBLE

1946   *Capriccio for Oboe and String Trio.* Premièred April 17, 1948, by Lois Wann, oboist, at the I.S.C.M. Forum Group, New York City.

1947   *The Great Wall of China.* Text by Franz Kafka. Soprano, flute, cello, and piano. ©1948 by *New Music.* Premièred May 1948 on the Alice Ditson Fund Concert at the Macmillan Theater, New York City.

1956   *A Guide to the Life Expectancy of a Rose.* Text by S. R. Tilley. Soprano, tenor, and chamber ensemble. Premièred May 16, 1956, by Bethany Beardslee, soprano, Earl Rogers, tenor, and Jacques Monod, conductor, New York City. Commissioned by the B. de Rothschild Foundation.

1959   *Valedictions* for mixed chorus, soprano, tenor, and ten instruments. Text by John Donne. Premièred May 1959 by the Schola Cantorum conducted by Hugh Ross, New York City.

1963   *The Confession.* Text by Jean Racine. Soprano, flute, strings, and piano. Premièred March 21, 1963, New York City.

1964   *Dreamscape* for piano, three flutes, cello, and percussion.

1965   *Concertino for Piano and Percussion Ensemble.* Premièred March 18, 1965, by the Paul Price Percussion Ensemble, Paul Price, conductor, and Vivian Fine, pianist.

1966   *Chamber Concerto for Cello and Six Instruments.* Premièred December 5, 1979, by George Finckel, cellist, at Windham College, Vermont.

1967   *Quintet for Trumpet, String Trio, and Harp.* Premièred June 3, 1967, at Washington, Connecticut. Commissioned by the Wykeham Rise School.

1971   *Sounds of the Nightingale* for soprano, female choral ensemble, and chamber orchestra. Premièred May 19, 1971, at Bennington College, Bennington, Vermont, Valerie Lamoree, soprano. Performed January 12, 1983, at Old First Church, San

Francisco. Reviewed by Heuwell Tircuit, "A Survey of Vivian Fine's Chamber Music Career," *San Francisco Chronicle,* January 11, 1983. Dedicated to the memory of Elinor Siegel.

1979   *For a Bust of Erik Satie* for soprano, mezzo soprano, narrator, and six instruments. Premièred May 11, 1979, at Bennington College.

Nightingales-Motet for Six Instruments. Premièred August 21, 1979, at Bennington, Vermont. Commissioned by the Chamber Music Conference and Composers Forum of the East.

1980   *Music for Flute (alto flute), Oboe (English horn), and Cello.* Premièred July 20, 1980, at Philadelphia. Commissioned by the Huntingdon Trio.

1987   *Ma's in Orbit* for violin, double bass, percussion, and piano. Premièred April 26, 1987, at the North American New Music Festival, State University at Buffalo, New York.

Dancing Winds for woodwind quintet. Recorded by the Catskill Woodwind Quintet, Redwood Records, ESC-48. Commissioned by the Catskill Woodwind Quintet.

In Memoriam: George Finckel for four cellos or multiples thereof. Premièred September 13, 1987, by an ensemble of sixteen celli conducted by Vivian Fine at Bennington College, Vermont.

1988   *Five Victorian Songs* for soprano, flute, clarinet, viola, and cello. Text by Christina Rossetti, Gerard Manley Hopkins, William Ernest Henley, and Elizabeth Barrett Browning. Premièred March 4, 1988, by The Capitol Chamber Artists at Green Mountain College, Poultney, Vermont. Commissioned by The Capitol Chamber Artists.

Asphodel for soprano, flute, clarinet, violin, viola, cello, percussion, and piano. Text by William Carlos Williams. Premièred April 10, 1989, by Musica Viva, Maria Tegzes, soprano, and Richard Pittman, conductor, at the Kathryn Bache Miller Theater, New York City. Commissioned by Musica Viva of Boston.

1991   *Hymns* for two pianos, French horn, and violoncello.

1993   *Canticles from the Other Side of the River* for flute, clarinet, percussion, piano, violin, and cello.

COMPOSITIONS FOR ORCHESTRA

1937   *The Race of Life.* Premièred January 23, 1938, by Doris Humphrey at New York City; first performance with orchestra conducted by Frederick Prausnitz on April 27, 1956, at the

Juilliard Dance Theater. Choreography by Doris Humphrey after a series of drawings by James Thurber; piano score première and later orchestral version.

1937   *Piece for Muted Strings (Elegiac Song) and Prelude for String Quartet* arranged for string orchestra. Premièred August 8, 1971, by conductor Jacob Glick at Lenox, Massachusetts.

1943–44   *Concertante for Piano and Orchestra.* Premièred by the Japan Philharmonic Orchestra, Akeo Watanabe, conductor, and Reiko Honsho, pianist, CRI 135 and in 1995 released on a compact disc, "American Masters: Vivian Fine" by CRI (CD 692) with jacket notes by Heidi Von Gunden.

1960   *Alcestis.* Choreographed and danced by Martha Graham. Premièred April 29, 1960, at New York City. Suite from ballet premièred November 5, 1983, at Bennington, Vermont, by conductor E. Guigui. Recorded by the Imperial Philharmonic of Tokyo conducted by William Strickland, CRI 145. Recording reviewed by Ralph Jones, *The New Records,* December 1961, 5. Commissioned by Martha Graham.

1967   *My Sledge and Hammer Ly Reclined* for chorus and orchestra. Premièred May 26, 1967, at Bennington, Vermont.

1971   *Sounds of the Nightingale* for soprano, female choral ensemble, and chamber orchestra. Premièred May 19, 1971, at Bennington College, Bennington, Vermont, Valerie Lamoree, soprano.

1975   *Meeting for Equal Rights 1866* for chorus, soloist, narrator, orchestra. Premièred April 23, 1976, by the Oratorio Society of New York conducted by Lyndon Woodside, Cooper Union, New York City. Commissioned by the Cooper Union, funded by The National Endowment for the Arts.

1976   *Sonnets for Baritone and Orchestra.* Text by Keats. Premièred December 5, 1976, at North Bennington, Vermont, by Louis Calabro conducting The Sage City Symphony. Commissioned by The Sage City Symphony.

1982   *Drama for Orchestra.* Premièred January 5, 1983, by the San Francisco Symphony conduced by Edo de Waart. Commissioned by Dr. and Mrs. Ralph I. Dorfman for the San Francisco Symphony's 1982–83 season. Reviewed by Robert Commanday, "Remarkable Individualism at the Symphony," *San Francisco Chronicle,* January 7, 1983, and Richard Pontzious, "Fine music not played well," *San Francisco Examiner,* January 6, 1983.

1984   *Poetic Fires* for orchestra and piano. Premièred February 21, 1985, by the American Composers Orchestra conducted by

Gunther Schuller, Vivian Fine, pianist, at Alice Tully Hall. Commissioned by the Koussevitsky Foundation.

1987   *After the Tradition* for orchestra. Premièred April 29, 1988, by the Bay Area Women's Philharmonic, JoAnn Falletta, conductor, at the First Congregational Church, Berkeley, California.

COMPOSITION FOR BAND

1988   *The Triple-Goddess* for concert band. Premièred April 22, 1989, by the Harvard University Band, Thomas Everett, conductor, at the Sander Theater, Cambridge, Massachusetts.

COMPOSITIONS FOR DANCE

1937   *The Race of Life* for piano and percussion. Premièred January 23, 1938, by Doris Humphrey at New York City; first performance with orchestra conducted by Frederick Prausnitz on April 27, 1956, at the Juilliard Dance Theater. Choreography by Doris Humphrey after a series of drawings by James Thurber.

1938   *Opus 51* for piano. Premièred on August 6, 1938, by Charles Weidman and Dance Company at the Fifth Bennington Dance Festival. Choreography by Charles Weidman.

1939   *Tragic Exodus* for baritone and piano. Vocalize. Premièred on February 19, 1939, at New York City. Choreography by Hanya Holm.
        They Too Are Exiles for piano duet. Premièred January 7, 1940, by Hanya Holm and Dance Company at New York City. Choreography by Hanya Holm.

1960   *Alcestis* for orchestra. Premièred April 29, 1960, by Martha Graham and Dance Company at New York City. Choreographed and danced by Martha Graham. Recorded by the Imperial Philharmonic of Tokyo conducted by William Strickland, CRI. Commissioned by Martha Graham.

1965   *My Song, My Enemy* for string quartet, piano, and percussion. Premièred August 14, 1965, at the American Dance Festival, New London, Connecticut. Choreographed by Jose Limón and conducted by Vivian Fine. Commissioned by the Rockefeller Foundation.

OPERA

1977   *Women in the Garden,* a chamber opera for five singers and nine instruments. Libretto by the composer from texts by the characters. Premièred February 12, 1978, by the Port Costa Players conducted by Alan Balter at the San Francisco Conservatory's Hellman Hall, San Francisco, California. Also performed on February 17 and 19 at the Laney College Theater in Oakland, California. Funded by The National Endowment for the Arts Grant. Reviewed by Charles Shere, "San Francisco: Port Costa Players: Fine premiere," *High Fidelity / Musical America,* June 1978, MA, 20–21; Stephanie Von Buchau, San Francisco/Bay Area," *Opera News,* July 1982, 34–35, and Robert Commanday, "A Plotless 'Garden' Gathering of Four Fantastic Personalities," *San Francisco Examiner & Chronicle,* February 12, 1978.

1994   *Memoirs of Uliana Rooney,* a multimedia chamber opera. Libretto by Sonya Friedman. Soprano, two baritones, and two female voices as chorus. Chamber orchestra of flute, clarinet, violin, cello, double bass, piano, and percussion (one player). Premièred February 1994 in New York City by the American Opera Projects Incorporated by Grethe Barret Holby, producer and artistic director, and Miriam Charney, pianist and music director. Commissioned by grants from Meet the Composer/Reader's Digest Commissioning Program, National Endowment for the Arts, and the Lila Wallace-Reader's Digest fund.

PUBLISHERS

Unless otherwise stated, Fine's compositions are available from Catamount Facsimile Edition.

Catamount Facsimile Edition
Box 245
Shaftsbury, Vt. 05262

Other publishers are:

Arsis Press
170 N.E. 33rd Street
Fort Lauderdale, Fla. 33334

Carl Fischer, Inc.
62 Cooper Square
New York, N.Y. 10003

Lawson-Gould Music Publishers, Inc.
250 West 57th Street
New York, N.Y. 10107

Lyra Music Co.
43 West 61st Street
New York, N.Y. 10023

Margun Music, Inc.
167 Dudley Road
Newton Centre, Mass. 02159

Discography

Alcestis. Imperial Philharmonic of Tokyo, William Strickland, conductor. CRI 145. Jacket notes by Don Jennings. CRI CD 692. Jacket notes by Heidi Von Gunden. Reviewed by Alfred Frankenstein, *High Fidelity,* January 1962, 77; William Flanagan, *HiFi/Stereo Review,* June 1962, 76; Arthur Cohn, *American Record Guide,* March 1962, 572–73; Dika Newlin, *Pan Pipes of Sigma Alpha Iota,* January 1962, 33; and Ralph Jones, *New Records,* December 1961, 5.

Concertante for Piano and Orchestra. Japan Philharmonic Symphony Orchestra, Akeo Watanabe, conducting; Reiko Honsho, piano. CRI 135. Jacket notes by William Flanagan. CRI CD 692. Jacket notes by Heidi Von Gunden.

Missa Brevis. American Academy and Institute of Arts and Letters Composers Award Record. Jan DeGaetani, mezzo-soprano; Eric Bartlett, David Finckel, Michael Finckel, Maxine Neuman, cellists. CRI SD 434. Jacket notes by Henry Brant. CRI CD 692. Jacket notes by Heidi Von Gunden. Reviewed by John Ditsky, *Fanfare,* July-August 1982, 120, and by Jay Donner, *New Records,* May 1982, 7.

Momenti. American Academy and Institute of Arts and Letters Composers Award Record. Lionel Nowak, pianist. CRI SD 434. Jacket notes by Henry Brant. CRI CD 692. Jacket notes by Heidi Von Gunden. Reviewed by John Ditsky, *Fanfare,* July-August 1982, 120, and by Jay Donner, *New Records,* May 1982, 7.

Paean. "Music From Bennington." Frank S. Baker, soloist; Eastman Brass Ensemble; Bennington Choral Ensemble; Vivian Fine, conductor. CRI SD 260. Reviewed by Alfred Frankenstein, "Recitals and Miscellany," *High Fidelity Magazine,* October 1971, 110 and 112, and Enos E. Shupp, Jr., *New Records,* August 1972, 6.

Quartet for Brass. American Academy and Institute of Arts and Letters Composers Award Record. Ronald K. Anderson and Allan Dean, trumpeters; David Jolley, French hornist; Lawrence Benz, bass trombonist. CRI SD 434. Jacket notes by Henry Brant. CRI CD 692. Jacket notes by Heidi Von Gunden. Reviewed by John Ditsky, *Fanfare,* July-August 1982, 120, and by Jay Donner, *New Records,* May 1982, 7.

Sinfonia and Fugato. New Music for Piano. Robert Helps. CRI SD 288. CRI CD 692. Jacket notes by Heidi Von Gunden. Reviewed by Lester Trimble, "Collections," *Stereo Review,* September 1972, 106.

Toccatas and Arias. 20th Century Harpsichord Music, Volume II. Barbara Harbach. Gasparo GSCD-266. Jacket notes by John Proffitt. Reviewed by Walter Simmons, *Fanfare,* November-December 1990, 435.

Bibliography

Ammer, Christine. *Unsung: A History of Women in American Music.* Westport, Conn.: Greenwood Press, 1980.

Anderson, E. Ruth. *Contemporary American Composers: A Biographical Dictionary.* 2d ed. Boston, Mass.: G. K. Hall, 1982.

Armer, Elinor. "A Conversation with Vivian Fine: Two Composers Talk Shop." *Strings,* March/April 1991, 73–78.

Au, Susan. *Ballet and Modern Dance.* London: Thames and Hudson, 1988.

Baker, Theodore. *The Concise Baker's Biographical Dictionary of Musicians.* New York: Schirmer, 1988.

Bauer, Marion. *Twentieth Century Music: How It Developed and How to Listen to It.* Rev. ed. New York: G. Putnam's Sons, 1937.

Beiswanger, George. "Music at the Bennington Festival." *Dance Observer,* August/September 1938, 102–4.

Berger, Arthur. "Yaddo Music Festival." *Daily Mirror,* May 3, 1932 (final edition), 13.

———. *Aaron Copland.* New York: Oxford University Press, 1953.

Block, Adrienne Fried, and Carol Neuls-Bates. *Women in American Music: A Bibliography of Music and Literature.* Westport, Conn.: Greenwood Press, 1979.

Boenke, Heidi. *Flute Music by Women Composers: An Annotated Catalog.* Westport, Conn.: Greenwood Press, 1988.

Boretz, Benjamin, and Edward T. Cone. *Perspectives on American Composers.* New York: Norton, 1971.

Bull, Storm. *Index to Biographies of Contemporary Composers.* Vol. 3. Metuchen, N.J.: Scarecrow Press, 1987.

Butler, Gervaise. "Reviews of the Month." *Dance Observer,* December 1938, 148–49.

Chanler, Theodore. "All-American." *Modern Music,* March/ April 1933, 160–62.

Chase, Gilbert, ed. *The American Composer Speaks.* Baton Rouge: Louisiana State University Press, 1966.

Child, Peter. "A Backward Glance: Music Activity in New England, c. 1930–1950—An Interview with Arthur Berger." In *Essays on Modern Music,* vol. 3, ed. Martin Brody. Boston, Mass.: League of Composers—International Society for Contemporary Music, 1987.

Church, Marjorie. "Y.M.H.A." *Dance Observer,* March 1939, 188.

Clarke, Garry. *Essays on American Music.* Westport, Conn.: Greenwood Press, 1977.

Code, Grant. "Dance Theatre of the WPA." *Dance Observer,* November 1939, 280–81, 290.

Cohen, Aaron. *International Discography of Women Composers.* Westport, Conn.: Greenwood Press, 1984.

———. *International Encyclopedia of Women Composers.* 2d ed. New York: Books and Music, 1987.

Commanday, Robert. "A Plotless 'Garden' Gathering of Four Fantastic Personalities." *San Francisco Chronicle,* February 12, 1978.

———. "Remarkable Individualism at the Symphony." *San Francisco Chronicle,* January 7, 1983.

———. "A Few Pearls among New-Music Offerings." *San Francisco Chronicle,* October 4, 1990.

Copland, Aaron, and Vivian Perlis. *Copland.* New York: St. Martin's, 1984.

Copland, Aaron, Roy Harris, Douglas Moore, Wallingford Riegger, Elie Siegmeister, Bernard Wagenaar, Marion Bauer, Goddard Lieberson, Quincy Porter, Roger Sessions, and Virgil Thomson. "A Manifesto from the American Composers Alliance." *Dance Observer,* May 1938, 68–69.

Cowell, Henry, ed. *American Composers on American Music.* New York: Frederick Ungar, 1933.

———. "Music at Bennington." *Dance Observer,* August–September 1941, 96–97.

Crawford, Richard, R. Allen Lott, and Carol J. Oja. A *Celebration of American Music: Words and Music in Honor of H. Wiley Hitchcock.* Ann Arbor, Mich.: The University of Michigan Press, 1990.

Dahlhaus, Carl. *Musik Lexikon.* London: Schott, 1972.

Driscoll, F. Paul. "Leading Ladies." *Opera News,* July 1992.

Dufourcq, N. *Larousse de la Musique.* Paris: Librairie Larousse, 1982.

Eagon, Angelo. *Catalog of Published Concert Music by American Composers,* 2d ed. Metuchen, N.J.: Scarecrow, 1969.

Ellison, Cori. "Breaking the Sound Barrier: How Women Finally Made Their Way to the Opera Stage." *Opera News,* July 1992, 14–17, 37.

Fábregas, Elisenda. "The Mostly Women Composers Festival." *International League of Women Composers Journal* (October 1994): 29.

Fine, Vivian. *Dance Perspectives* 16 (1963): 8–11.

Fruchter, Rena. "American Women Focus of Concert." *New York Times,* February 26, 1989.

Gaume, Matilda. *Ruth Crawford Seeger: Memoirs, Memories, Music.* Metuchen, N.J.: Scarecrow Press, 1986

Gilbert, Steven E. "'The Ultra-Modern Idiom': A Survey of New Music." *Perspectives of New Music,* Fall/Winter 1973–Spring/Summer 1974, 310.

Gilfond, Henry. "Bennington Festival." *Dance Observer,* August–September 1938, 100–102.

———. "Summing Up." *Dance Observer,* June–July 1939, 238.

———. "Hanya Holm and Group." *Dance Observer,* February 1940, 23.

Graham, Martha. *The Notebooks of Martha Graham.* New York: Harcourt Brace Jovanovich, 1973.

Greene, Frank, comp. *Composers on Record: An Index to Bibliographical Information on 14,000 Composers Whose Music Has Been Recorded.* Metuchen, N.J.: Scarecrow Press, 1985.

Harrison, Lou. "Forum Group Music: Contemporary Music Society Concert at Times Hall." *New York Herald Tribune,* April 17, 1946.

Henahan, Donal. "Concert." *New York Times,* April 12, 1973.

———. "Concert: Oratorio Society Sings Equal-Rights Cantata." *New York Times,* May 22, 1976.

Hinson, Maurice. *Guide to the Pianist's Repertoire.* 2d ed. Bloomington: Indiana University Press.

Hixon, Don L., and Don Henesse. *Women in Music: A Biobibliography.* Metuchen, N.J.: Scarecrow, 1975.

Howard, John Tasker. *A Short History of Music in America.* New York: Thomas Y. Crowell, 1957.

Humphrey, Doris. "Music for an American Dance." *Bulletin of the American Composers Alliance* 8/1 (1958): 4–5.

Imbrie, Andrew. "Roger Sessions: In Honor of His Sixty-fifth Birthday." *Perspectives on American Composers.* New York: Norton, 1971.

"Interview with Doris Humphrey." *Dance Observer,* May 1938, 69.

Jones, Leslie. "The Solo Piano Music of Vivian Fine." Doctor of musical arts thesis, The College-Conservatory of Music of the University of Cincinnati, 1994.

Karp, Vivian, and Benjamin Karp, eds. *Louis Rapkine 1904–1948.* North Bennington, Vt.: The Orpheus Press, 1988.

Kozinn, Allan. "Review/Piano: Concentration and Finger Power." *New York Times,* February 1, 1987.

———. "Pamela Frank, a Violinist, in New York Recital Debut." *New York Times,* April 22, 1990.

LePage, Jane Weiner. *Women Composers, Conductors, and Musicians of the Twentieth Century: Selected Biographies: Vol. II.* Metuchen, N.J.: Scarecrow Press, 1983.

Levant, Oscar. *A Smattering of Ignorance.* New York: Garden City Publishing Co., 1942.

Lewis, Daniel. *The Illustrated Dance Technique of Jose Limón.* New York: Harper and Row, 1984.

Locke, Ralph. "What Are These Women Doing in Opera?" *Opera News,* July 1992, 34–37.

Maynard, Olga. *American Modern Dancers: The Pioneers.* Boston, Mass.: Little, Brown and Company, 1965.

McCausland, Elizabeth. "Hanya Holm and Concert Group." *Dance Observer,* March 1939, 186–87.

Mead, Rita. *Henry Cowell's New Music, 1925–1936: The Society, the Music Editions, and the Records.* Ann Arbor, Mich.: UMI Research Press, 1981.

Meggett, Joan M. *Keyboard Music by Women Composers: A Catalog and Bibliography.* Westport, Conn.: Greenwood Press, 1981.

Meyer, Alfred H. "Yaddo—A May Festival." *Modern Music,* May–June 1932, 172–76.

Mitgang, Herbert. "Cultural Prizes Are Conferred by American Academy Institute." *New York Times,* May 12, 1980.

Molyneux, Anna C. "Paul Boepple and the Dalcroze School." *Dance Observer,* January 1940, 5.

Morton, Brian, and Pamela Collins, ed. *Contemporary Composers.* Chicago: St. James Press, 1992.

Newcomb, Theodore, Kathryn E. Koenig, Richard Flacks, and Donald Warwick. *Persistence and Change: Bennington College and Its Students after Twenty-five Years.* New York: John Wiley and Sons, 1967.

New York Times, "Arts and Letters Body Elects 11 New Members." April 4, 1980.

Nichols, Janet. *Women Music Makers: An Introduction to Women Composers.* New York: Walker and Co., 1992.

O'Donnell, Mary. "Doris Humphrey-Charles Weidman." *Dance Observer,* March 1938, 38.

Oja, Carol J., ed. *American Music Recordings: A Discography of 20th-Century U. S. Composers.* New York: Institute for Studies in American Music, 1982.

Olmstead, Andrea. *Rogers Sessions and His Music.* Ann Arbor, Mich.: UMI Research Press, 1985.

———. *Conversations with Roger Sessions.* Boston, Mass.: Northeastern University Press, 1987.

Orme, Frederic L. "These Were the Moderns—Yesterday." *American Dancer,* January 1939, 16–17.

———. "Charles Weidman: The Master Mime." *American Dancer,* November 1939, 11, 34.

Parmenter, Ross. "Music: A New Concert-Giving Group." *New York Times,* May 16, 1956.

Pendle, Karin. *Women and Music: A History.* Bloomington: Indiana University Press, 1991.

———. "Lost Voices." *Opera News,* July 1992, 18, 19, 44.

Percival, John. *Experimental Dance.* New York: Universe Books, 1971.

Pontzious, Richard. "Fine music not played well," *San Francisco Examiner,* January 6, 1983.

Pool, Jeannie G. *Women in Music History: A Research Guide.* New York: The author, 1977.

Reis, Claire. *Composers in America.* New York: Macmillan, 1947.

Riegger, Wallingford. "The Music of Vivian Fine." *Bulletin of the American Composers Alliance* 8/1 (1958): 2–4.

Roberts, Peter Deane. *Modernism in Russian Piano Music: Skriabin, Prokofiev, and Their Russian Contemporaries.* Bloomington: Indiana University Press, 1993.

Rosenfeld, Paul. *Discoveries of a Music Critic.* New York: Vienna House, 1972.

Rudhyar, Dane. "The Companionate Marriage of Music and Dance." *Dance Observer,* March 1938.

Sabin, Robert. "Aaron Copland on Music for the Dance." *Dance Observer,* February 1942, 26.

———. "Reviews of the Month: Martha Graham and Company." *Dance Observer,* June-July 1960, 85–86.

Sadie, Stanley. *Norton/Grove Concise Encyclopedia of Music.* New York: Norton, 1988.

Saylor, Bruce. "The Tempering of Henry Cowell's 'Dissonant Counterpoint.'" *Essays on Modern Music.* Vol. 2, nos. 1, 2, 3, ed. Martin Brody. Boston, Mass.: League of Composers—International Society for Contemporary Music, 1984.

Schein, Eugenie. "The Dance, the Y.M.H.A. and Mr. Kolodney." *Dance Observer,* December 1941, 133.

Schubart, Mark. "Young Composers Offer New Works Here: Present-day Writers Show to Advantage," *New York Times,* April 17, 1946.

Sessions, Roger. *The Musical Experience of Composer, Performer, Listener.* Princeton, N.J.: Princeton University Press, 1950.

———. *Harmonic Practice.* New York: Harcourt, Brace and World, 1951.

———. "To the Editor." *Perspectives on American Composers.* Ed. Benjamin Boretz and Edward T. Cone. New York: Norton, 1971.

Shackelford, Rudy. "The Yaddo Festivals of American Music, 1932–1952." *Perspectives of New Music,* Fall-Winter 1978, 92–125.

Sherbon, Elizabeth. "Doris Humphrey, Charles Weidman and Concert Groups." *Dance Observer,* January 1939, 163.

———. "Hanya Holm and Group." *Dance Observer,* April 1939, 204.

Shere, Charles. "San Francisco: Port Costa Players: Fine premiere." *High Fidelity/Musical America,* June 1978, MA, 20–21.

Siegel, Marcia. *Days on Earth: The Dance of Doris Humphrey.* New Haven, Conn.: Yale University Press, 1987.

Simons, Stacy. "Vivian Fine, Netty Simons, and Nancy Van de Vate: A Singer's Look at Three American Composers." Doctoral thesis at the University of Illinois, 1990.

Slonimsky, Nicolas. *Abridged Version of Baker's Biographical Dictionary of Musicians.* 7th ed. New York: Schirmer Books, 1971.

———. *Supplement to Music Since 1900.* New York: Scribner's Sons, 1986.

Sorell, Walter. *Hanya Holm: The Biography of an Artist.* Middletown, Conn.: Wesleyan University Press, 1969.

Spackman, Stephen. *Wallingford Riegger: Two Essays in Musical Biography.* New York: Institute for Studies in American Music, 1982.

Stone, Kurt. "Vivian Fine." *New Grove Dictionary of Music and Musicians.* London: Macmillan, 1980.

Swados, Elizabeth. *Listening Out Loud: Becoming a Composer.* New York: Harper and Row, 1988.

Thompson, Oscar, ed. *The International Cyclopedia of Music and Musicians.* New York: Dodd, Mead, and Company, 1975.

Thomson, Virgil. *American Music Since 1910.* New York: Holt, Rinehart, and Winston, 1970, 1971.

Tick, Judith. *Ruth Crawford Seeger: A Composer's Search for American Music.* New York: Oxford University Press, 1987, 59–63, 72, 76, 86, 89, 95, 106, 113, 118–24, 127, 131, 133, 150, 159, 175, 181–83, 191, 198, 222, 224, 226–27, 390 n 83.

Tircuit, Heuwell. "A Survey of Vivian Fine's Chamber Music Career." *San Francisco Chronicle,* January 11, 1983.

Upton, William T. "Aspects of the Modern Art-Song." *Musical Quarterly,* January 1938, 12, 16–22.

Vercoe, Elizabeth. "Interview with Composer Vivian Fine." *International League of Women Composers Journal* (June 1992): 18–23.

Vinton, John. *Dictionary of Contemporary Music.* New York: Dutton, 1974.

Vitak, Albertina. "Dance Events Reviewed." *American Dancer,* January 1939, 23, 43.

Von Buchau, Stephanie. "Room at the Top." *Opera News,* July 1992, 8–12, 44.

———. "Reports: US—San Francisco/Bay Area." *Opera News,* July 1982, 34–35.

Waite, Marjorie Peabody. *Yaddo: Yesterday and Today.* Saratoga Springs, N.Y.: Argus Press, 1933.

Whiteside, Abby. *Indispensables of Piano Playing.* New York: Coleman–Ross Company, 1955.

———. *Mastering the Chopin Etudes and Other Essays.* New York: Charles Scribner's Son, 1969.

Wilson, Derek. *Rothschild: A Story of Wealth and Power.* London: André Deutsch, 1988.

Wood, Ralph W. "Modern Counterpoint." *Music and Letters,* July 1932, 312–18.

Zuck, Barbara A. *A History of Musical Americanism.* Ann Arbor: University of Michigan Research Press, 1980.

Index

About the Author

Heidi Von Gunden holds a Ph.D in music from the University of California at San Diego. She is an associate professor at the University of Illinois, Champaign-Urbana. Her publications include *The Music of Pauline Oliveros* (Scarecrow, 1983), *The Music of Ben Johnston* (Scarecrow, 1986), and *The Music of Lou Harrison* (Scarecrow, 1995). In addition, Von Gunden has published several compositions and contributed theoretical writings and analyses to the *College Music Symposium, Neuland, Perspectives of New Music,* and the *International League of Women Composers Journal.*